SYNCHRONICITY

An Acausal Connecting
Principle

from

The Collected Works of C. G. Jung

VOLUME 8

BOLLINGEN SERIES XX

SYNCHRONICITY

An Acausal Connecting
Principle

C. G. JUNG

TRANSLATED BY R. F. C. HULL

BOLLINGEN SERIES

PRINCETON UNIVERSITY PRESS

First Princeton/Bollingen Paperback Edition, 1973

Extracted from *The Structure and Dynamics of the Psyche*, Vol. 8 of the *Collected Works of C. G. Jung*. All the volumes comprising the *Collected Works* constitute number XX in Bollingen Series, under the editorship of Herbert Read (d. 1968), Michael Fordham, and Gerhard Adler; executive editor, William McGuire.

Princeton University Press books are printed on acid-free paper and meet the guidelines for permanence and durability of the Committee on Production Guidelines for Book Longevity of the Council on Library Resources

18   17   16   15   14   13   12

LIBRARY OF CONGRESS CATALOG CARD NUMBER: 73-11838
ISBN 0-691-01794-8
MANUFACTURED IN THE UNITED STATES OF AMERICA

EDITORIAL PREFACE

When a young man, Jung saw a solid oak table suddenly split right across. Soon afterwards a strong steel knife broke in pieces for no apparent reason.[1] His superstitious mother, who also witnessed both these events, looked at him significantly, and this made Jung wonder what it was all about. Later he learned that some of his relatives had been attending seances with a medium: they had been wanting to ask him to join them.

For Jung and his mother these occurrences, apparently separate, became linked together in a meaningful way. It was unlikely that the split table and broken knife were caused by the thoughts of his relatives or that the medium was seeking to impress him magically with her powers. However, that these happenings stimulated him to join in the seances and that he subsequently undertook research into occultism[2] bear witness to their effect upon him.

Jung introduced the idea of synchronicity to strip off the fantasy, magic, and superstition which surround and are provoked by unpredictable, startling, and impressive events that, like these, appear to be connected. They are simply "meaningful coincidences." In spite of this almost stark definition, Jung's idea has been attacked or applauded in the most unsuitable ways—probably the fate of most simple and direct statements in the highly controversial field of parapsychology. But Jung introduced a puzzling complication: in support of his idea he cited J. B. Rhine's researches. Rhine's statistical analysis of

[1] Jung tells the story in *Memories, Dreams, Reflections* (New York and London, 1963), pp. 105/108, and in a letter to Professor J. B. Rhine, 27 Nov. 1934, in *C. G. Jung: Letters*, ed. Gerhard Adler in collaboration with Aniela Jaffé, vol. 1 (Princeton and London, 1973), pp. 180f., with a photograph of the knife.
[2] The research led to Jung's dissertation for the M.D. degree, *Zur Psychologie und Pathologie sogenannter occulter Phänomene* (Leipzig, 1902) = "On the Psychology and Pathology of So-called Occult Phenomena," Coll. Works, vol. 2. Also see the accounts in *Memories, Dreams, Reflections*, pp. 106f./109f. and in the letter to Rhine cited above.

psychokinetic experiments led him to conclude a causal relation between the subjects' "guessing" the numbers on cards and the actual numbers printed on them.

It might be maintained that it is of no significance whether the separate events in a meaningful sequence are caused or not, for it is the meaning of the entire group, the sequence, that Jung emphasized. This, however, was not Jung's idea; and so to record his astrological experiment in which no correlation was statistically significant becomes relevant, for it may be held that statistics can decide whether the meaningful patterns he saw were acausal. Whether "acausal" and "chance" are the same may be debated, but whether they are or not, it is frequently thought that the use of statistics in the astrological experiment is proof for the existence of meaningful coincidences. This could never be.

In the monograph here published, the simple idea of synchronicity is extended by Jung, with all the apparatus of his ingenious mind and great erudition, in striking and thought-provoking ways. The work is highly characteristic of Jung's insistence that because data are irrational they should not be dismissed, but rather that attempts should be made to integrate them by whatever means may be at hand. In this instance he evolved the idea of synchronicity, and it deserves assessment by all investigators in the various fields on which it impinges, from parapsychology to the psychology of unconscious structures and processes.

London, 1973   MICHAEL FORDHAM

*

Late in his life, Jung traced his idea of synchronicity to the influence of Albert Einstein, who held a professorship in Zurich in 1909–10 and again in 1912–13. Jung wrote, "Professor Einstein was my guest on several occasions at dinner. . . . These were very early days when Einstein was developing his first theory of relativity, [and] it was he who first started me off thinking about a possible relativity of time as well as space, and their psychic conditionality. More than thirty years later, this stimulus led to my relation with the physicist Professor W. Pauli and to my thesis of psychic synchronicity."[3]

Jung first used the term "synchronicity" only in 1930, in his memorial address for Richard Wilhelm,[4] the translator of the *I Ching, or Book of Changes.*[5] Jung was seeking to explain the *modus operandi* of the *I Ching,* which he had first come across in the early 1920's in an English translation by James Legge (1882) but, as he said, came to understand only when he read Wilhelm's version.

He referred to synchronicity again in his "Tavistock Lectures" in London, 1935: ". . . a peculiar principle active in the world so that things happen together somehow and behave as if they were the same, and yet for us they are not."[6] Again in the Lectures he equated it with the Chinese concept of Tao.[7]

Years later, in his foreword (written before 1950) to the Wilhelm/Baynes translation of the *I Ching,* Jung gave an exposition of the principle of synchronicity.[8] He was already preparing an extended monograph, but his first formal presentation of the theory was a brief lecture—his last—at the Eranos Conference of 1951 at Ascona, Switzerland.[9] The monograph was published the following year, together with a monograph by Pauli on "The Influence of Archetypal Ideas on the Scientific Theories of Johannes Kepler."[10] An English translation of the volume, with corrections and extensive revisions by Jung, was subsequently published.[11] Jung's monograph appeared in vol. 8 of the Collected Works in 1960 and, with further revisions by the translator, in the second edition of vol. 8, 1969. It is the latter version that is published here.

3 Letter to Dr. Carl Seelig, 25 Feb. 1953, in *C. G. Jung: Letters,* vol. 2 (1974).

4 Included in Jung and Wilhelm, *The Secret of the Golden Flower,* tr. Cary F. Baynes (London and New York, 1931). See "Richard Wilhelm: In Memoriam," Coll. Works, vol. 15, pars. 81ff.

5 See the Richard Wilhelm tr. rendered into English by Cary F. Baynes (New York and London, 1950; 3rd edition, Princeton and London, 1967).

6 *Analytical Psychology: Its Theory and Practice* (London and New York, 1968), p. 36. (To be included in Coll. Works, vol. 18.)

7 Ibid., p. 76.

8 In the 3rd edition, pp. xxivff.; also in Coll. Works, vol. 11, pars. 972ff.

9 In the present vol., pars. 969ff.

10 *Naturerklärung und Psyche* (Studien aus dem C. G. Jung-Institut, IV; Zurich, 1952).

11 *The Interpretation of Nature and the Psyche,* tr. R. F. C. Hull and Priscilla Silz (New York and London, 1955).

TABLE OF CONTENTS

SYNCHRONICITY: AN ACAUSAL CONNECTING PRINCIPLE

[Translated from "Synchronizität als ein Prinzip akausaler Zusammenhänge," which, together with a monograph by Professor W. Pauli entitled "Der Einfluss archetypischer Vorstellungen auf die Bildung naturwissenschaftlicher Theorien bei Kepler," formed the volume *Naturerklärung und Psyche* (Studien aus dem C. G. Jung-Institut, IV; Zurich, 1952). This volume was translated as *The Interpretation of Nature and the Psyche* (New York [Bollingen Series LI] and London, 1955), with corrections and extensive revisions by Professor Jung in his Chapter 2, "An Astrological Experiment." These important alterations were not, however, incorporated in the republication of the monograph in the Swiss *Gesammelte Werke*, Volume 8: *Die Dynamik des Unbewussten* (Zurich, 1967), which preserves the original 1952 version unchanged. The monograph is here republished with additional revisions by the Editors and the translator, with the aim of further clarifying the difficult exposition while retaining the author's substance. (The chief revisions occur in pars. 856, 880, 883, 890, 893, 895, and 901. Figs. 2 and 3 have been redrawn.)

[The brief essay "On Synchronicity" printed in the appendix to Part VII, *infra*, was an earlier (1951) and more popular version of the present work. Here it replaces a brief "Résumé" written by the author for the 1955 version of the monograph.—EDITORS.]

FOREWORD

816 In writing this paper I have, so to speak, made good a promise which for many years I lacked the courage to fulfil. The difficulties of the problem and its presentation seemed to me too great; too great the intellectual responsibility without which such a subject cannot be tackled; too inadequate, in the long run, my scientific training. If I have now conquered my hesitation and at last come to grips with my theme, it is chiefly because my experiences of the phenomenon of synchronicity have multiplied themselves over decades, while on the other hand my researches into the history of symbols, and of the fish symbol in particular, brought the problem ever closer to me, and finally because I have been alluding to the existence of this phenomenon on and off in my writings for twenty years without discussing it any further. I would like to put a temporary end to this unsatisfactory state of affairs by trying to give a consistent account of everything I have to say on this subject. I hope it will not be construed as presumption on my part if I make uncommon demands on the open-mindedness and goodwill of the reader. Not only is he expected to plunge into regions of human experience which are dark, dubious, and hedged about with prejudice, but the intellectual difficulties are such as the treatment and elucidation of so abstract a subject must inevitably entail. As anyone can see for himself after reading a

3

few pages, there can be no question of a complete description and explanation of these complicated phenomena, but only an attempt to broach the problem in such a way as to reveal some of its manifold aspects and connections, and to open up a very obscure field which is philosophically of the greatest importance. As a psychiatrist and psychotherapist I have often come up against the phenomena in question and could convince myself how much these inner experiences meant to my patients. In most cases they were things which people do not talk about for fear of exposing themselves to thoughtless ridicule. I was amazed to see how many people have had experiences of this kind and how carefully the secret was guarded. So my interest in this problem has a human as well as a scientific foundation.

817   In the performance of my work I had the support of a number of friends who are mentioned in the text. Here I would like to express my particular thanks to Dr. Liliane Frey-Rohn, for her help with the astrological material.

4

1. EXPOSITION

818   The discoveries of modern physics have, as we know, brought about a significant change in our scientific picture of the world, in that they have shattered the absolute validity of natural law and made it relative. Natural laws are *statistical* truths, which means that they are completely valid only when we are dealing with macrophysical quantities. In the realm of very small quantities prediction becomes uncertain, if not impossible, because very small quantities no longer behave in accordance with the known natural laws.

819   The philosophical principle that underlies our conception of natural law is *causality*. But if the connection between cause and effect turns out to be only statistically valid and only relatively true, then the causal principle is only of relative use for explaining natural processes and therefore presupposes the existence of one or more other factors which would be necessary for an explanation. This is as much as to say that the connection of events may in certain circumstances be other than causal, and requires another principle of explanation.[1]

820   We shall naturally look round in vain in the macrophysical world for acausal events, for the simple reason that we cannot imagine events that are connected non-causally and are capable

[1] [Other than, or supplementary to, the laws of chance.—EDITORS.]

of a non-causal explanation. But that does not mean that such events do not exist. Their existence—or at least their possibility —follows logically from the premise of statistical truth.

821   The experimental method of inquiry aims at establishing regular events which can be repeated. Consequently, unique or rare events are ruled out of account. Moreover, the experiment imposes limiting conditions on nature, for its aim is to force her to give answers to questions devised by man. Every answer of nature is therefore more or less influenced by the kind of questions asked, and the result is always a hybrid product. The so-called "scientific view of the world" based on this can hardly be anything more than a psychologically biased partial view which misses out all those by no means unimportant aspects that cannot be grasped statistically. But, to grasp these unique or rare events at all, we seem to be dependent on equally "unique" and individual descriptions. This would result in a chaotic collection of curiosities, rather like those old natural history cabinets where one finds, cheek by jowl with fossils and anatomical monsters in bottles, the horn of a unicorn, a mandragora manikin, and a dried mermaid. The descriptive sciences, and above all biology in the widest sense, are familiar with these "unique" specimens, and in their case only *one* example of an organism, no matter how unbelievable it may be, is needed to establish its existence. At any rate numerous observers will be able to convince themselves, on the evidence of their own eyes, that such a creature does in fact exist. But where we are dealing with ephemeral events which leave no demonstrable traces behind them except fragmentary memories in people's minds, then a single witness no longer suffices, nor would several witnesses be enough to make a unique event appear absolutely credible. One has only to think of the notorious unreliability of eye-witness accounts. In these circumstances we are faced with the necessity of finding out whether the apparently unique event is really unique in our recorded experience, or whether the same or similar events are not to be found elsewhere. Here the *consensus omnium* plays a very important role psychologically, though empirically it is somewhat doubtful, for only in exceptional cases does the *consensus omnium* prove to be of value in establishing facts. The empiricist will not leave it out of account, but will do better not to rely on it. Absolutely unique and ephem-

eral events whose existence we have no means of either denying or proving can never be the object of empirical science; rare events might very well be, provided that there was a sufficient number of reliable individual observations. The so-called *possibility* of such events is of no importance whatever, for the criterion of what is possible in any age is derived from that age's rationalistic assumptions. There are no "absolute" natural laws to whose authority one can appeal in support of one's prejudices. The most that can fairly be demanded is that the number of individual observations shall be as high as possible. If this number, statistically considered, falls within the limits of chance expectation, then it has been statistically proved that it was a question of chance; but no *explanation* has thereby been furnished. There has merely been an exception to the rule. When, for instance, the number of symptoms indicating a complex falls below the probable number of disturbances to be expected during the association experiment, this is no justification for assuming that no complex exists. But that did not prevent the reaction disturbances from being regarded earlier as pure chance.[2]

822   Although, in biology especially, we move in a sphere where causal explanations often seem very unsatisfactory—indeed, well-nigh impossible—we shall not concern ourselves here with the problems of biology, but rather with the question whether there may not be some general field where acausal events not only are possible but are found to be actual facts.

823   Now, there is in our experience an immeasurably wide field whose extent forms, as it were, the counterbalance to the domain of causality. This is the world of chance, where a chance event seems causally unconnected with the coinciding fact. So we shall have to examine the nature and the whole idea of chance a little more closely. Chance, we say, must obviously be susceptible of some causal explanation and is only called "chance" or "coincidence" because its causality has not yet been discovered. Since we have an inveterate conviction of the absolute validity of causal law, we regard this explanation of chance as being quite adequate. But if the causal principle is only relatively valid, then it follows that even though in the vast majority of

2 [Cf. Jung, *Studies in Word Association.*—EDITORS.]

cases an apparently chance series can be causally explained, there must still remain a number of cases which do not show any causal connection. We are therefore faced with the task of sifting chance events and separating the acausal ones from those that can be causally explained. It stands to reason that the number of causally explicable events will far exceed those suspected of acausality, for which reason a superficial or prejudiced observer may easily overlook the relatively rare acausal phenomena. As soon as we come to deal with the problem of chance the need for a statistical evaluation of the events in question forces itself upon us.

824   It is not possible to sift the empirical material without a criterion of distinction. How are we to recognize acausal combinations of events, since it is obviously impossible to examine all chance happenings for their causality? The answer to this is that acausal events may be expected most readily where, on closer reflection, a causal connection appears to be inconceivable. As an example I would cite the "duplication of cases" which is a phenomenon well known to every doctor. Occasionally there is a trebling or even more, so that Kammerer [3] can speak of a "law of series," of which he gives a number of excellent examples. In the majority of such cases there is not even the remotest probability of a causal connection between the coinciding events. When for instance I am faced with the fact that my tram ticket bears the same number as the theatre ticket which I buy immediately afterwards, and I receive that same evening a telephone call during which the same number is mentioned again as a telephone number, then a causal connection between these events seems to me improbable in the extreme, although it is obvious that each must have its own causality. I know, on the other hand, that chance happenings have a tendency to fall into aperiodic groupings—necessarily so, because otherwise there would be only a periodic or regular arrangement of events which would by definition exclude chance.

825   Kammerer holds that though "runs" [4] or successions of chance events are not subject to the operation of a common cause,[5] i.e., are acausal, they are nevertheless an expression of

3 Paul Kammerer, *Das Gesetz der Serie*.   4 Ibid., p. 130.
5 Pp. 36, 93f., 102f.

inertia—the property of persistence.[6] The simultaneity of a "run of the same thing side by side" he explains as "imitation." [7] Here he contradicts himself, for the run of chance has not been "removed outside the realm of the explicable," [8] but, as we would expect, is included within it and is consequently reducible, if not to a common cause, then at least to several causes. His concepts of seriality, imitation, attraction, and inertia belong to a causally conceived view of the world and tell us no more than that the run of chance corresponds to statistical and mathematical probability.[9] Kammerer's factual material contains nothing but runs of chance whose only "law" is probability; in other words, there is no apparent reason why he should look behind them for anything else. But for some obscure reason he does look behind them for something more than mere probability warrants—for a *law of seriality* which he would like to introduce as a principle coexistent with causality and finality. This tendency, as I have said, is in no way justified by his material. I can only explain this obvious contradiction by supposing that he had a dim but fascinated intuition of an acausal arrangement and combination of events, probably because, like all thoughtful and sensitive natures, he could not escape the peculiar impression which runs of chance usually make on us, and therefore, in accordance with his scientific disposition, took the bold step of postulating an acausal seriality on the basis of empirical material that lay within the limits of probability. Unfortunately he did not attempt a quantitative evaluation of seriality. Such an undertaking would undoubtedly have thrown up questions that are difficult to answer. The investigation of individual cases serves well enough for the purpose of general orientation, but only quantitative evaluation or the statistical method promises results in dealing with chance.

826   Chance groupings or series seem, at least to our present way

6 "The law of series is an expression of the inertia of the objects involved in its repetitions (i.e., producing the series). The far greater inertia of a complex of objects and forces (as compared to that of a single object or force) explains the persistence of an identical constellation and the emergence, connected therewith, of repetitions over long periods of time" (p. 117).   7 P. 130.   8 P. 94.

9 [The term "probability" therefore refers to the probability on a chance hypothesis (Null Hypothesis). This is the sense in which the term is most often used in this paper.—EDITORS.]

of thinking, to be meaningless, and to fall as a general rule within the limits of probability. There are, however, incidents whose "chancefulness" seems open to doubt. To mention but one example out of many, I noted the following on April 1, 1949: Today is Friday. We have fish for lunch. Somebody happens to mention the custom of making an "April fish" of someone. That same morning I made a note of an inscription which read: "Est homo totus medius *piscis* ab imo." In the afternoon a former patient of mine, whom I had not seen for months, showed me some extremely impressive pictures of fish which she had painted in the meantime. In the evening I was shown a piece of embroidery with fish-like sea-monsters in it. On the morning of April 2 another patient, whom I had not seen for many years, told me a dream in which she stood on the shore of a lake and saw a large fish that swam straight towards her and landed at her feet. I was at this time engaged on a study of the fish symbol in history. Only one of the persons mentioned here knew anything about it.

827   The suspicion that this must be a case of *meaningful coincidence,* i.e., an acausal connection, is very natural. I must own that this run of events made a considerable impression on me. It seemed to me to have a certain numinous quality.[10] In such circumstances we are inclined to say, "That cannot be mere chance," without knowing what exactly we are saying. Kammerer would no doubt have reminded me of his "seriality." The strength of an impression, however, proves nothing against the fortuitous coincidence of all these fishes. It is, admittedly, exceedingly odd that the fish theme recurs no less than six times within twenty-four hours. But one must remember that fish on Friday is the usual thing, and on April 1 one might very easily think of the April fish. I had at that time been working on the fish symbol for several months. Fishes frequently occur as symbols of unconscious contents. So there is no possible justification for seeing in this anything but a chance grouping. Runs or

---

[10] The numinosity of a series of chance happenings grows in proportion to the number of its terms. Unconscious—probably archetypal—contents are thereby constellated, which then give rise to the impression that the series has been "caused" by these contents. Since we cannot conceive how this could be possible without recourse to positively magical categories, we generally let it go at the bare impression.

series which are composed of quite ordinary occurrences must for the present be regarded as fortuitous.[11] However wide their range may be, they must be ruled out as acausal connections. It is, therefore, generally assumed that all coincidences are lucky hits and do not require an acausal interpretation.[12] This assumption can, and indeed must, be regarded as true so long as proof is lacking that their incidence exceeds the limits of probability. Should this proof be forthcoming, however, it would prove at the same time that there are genuinely non-causal combinations of events for whose explanation we should have to postulate a factor incommensurable with causality. We should then have to assume that events in general are related to one another on the one hand as causal chains, and on the other hand by a kind of *meaningful cross-connection.*

828   Here I should like to draw attention to a treatise of Schopenhauer's, "On the Apparent Design in the Fate of the Individual," [13] which originally stood godfather to the views I am now developing. It deals with the "simultaneity of the causally unconnected, which we call 'chance'." [14] Schopenhauer illustrates this simultaneity by a geographical analogy, where the parallels represent the cross-connection between the meridians, which are thought of as causal chains.[15]

11 As a pendant to what I have said above, I should like to mention that I wrote these lines sitting by the lake. Just as I had finished this sentence, I walked over to the sea-wall and there lay a dead fish, about a foot long, apparently uninjured. No fish had been there the previous evening. (Presumably it had been pulled out of the water by a bird of prey or a cat.) The fish was the seventh in the series.

12 We find ourselves in something of a quandary when it comes to making up our minds about the phenomenon which Stekel calls the "compulsion of the name." What he means by this is the sometimes quite grotesque coincidence between a man's name and his peculiarities or profession. For instance Herr Gross (Mr. Grand) suffers from delusions of grandeur, Herr Kleiner (Mr. Small) has an inferiority complex. The Altmann sisters marry men twenty years older than themselves. Herr Feist (Mr. Stout) is the Food Minister, Herr Rosstäuscher (Mr. Horsetrader) is a lawyer, Herr Kalberer (Mr. Calver) is an obstetrician, Herr Freud (joy) champions the pleasure-principle, Herr Adler (eagle) the will-to-power, Herr Jung (young) the idea of rebirth, and so on. Are these the whimsicalities of chance, or the suggestive effects of the name, as Stekel seems to suggest, or are they "meaningful coincidences"? ("Die Verpflichtung des Namens," 110ff.)

13 *Parerga und Paralipomena*, I, ed. by von Koeber. [Cf. the trans. by David Irvine, to which reference is made for convenience, though not quoted here.]

14 Ibid., p. 40. [Irvine, p. 41.]   15 P. 39. [Irvine, pp. 39f.]

All the events in a man's life would accordingly stand in two fundamentally different kinds of connection: firstly, in the objective, causal connection of the natural process; secondly, in a subjective connection which exists only in relation to the individual who experiences it, and which is thus as subjective as his own dreams. . . . That both kinds of connection exist simultaneously, and the selfsame event, although a link in two totally different chains, nevertheless falls into place in both, so that the fate of one individual invariably fits the fate of the other, and each is the hero of his own drama while simultaneously figuring in a drama foreign to him— this is something that surpasses our powers of comprehension, and can only be conceived as possible by virtue of the most wonderful pre-established harmony.[16]

In his view "the subject of the great dream of life . . . is but one," [17] the transcendental Will, the *prima causa*, from which all causal chains radiate like meridian lines from the poles and, because of the circular parallels, stand to one another in a meaningful relationship of simultaneity.[18] Schopenhauer believed in the absolute determinism of the natural process and furthermore in a first cause. There is nothing to warrant either assumption. The first cause is a philosophical mythologem which is only credible when it appears in the form of the old paradox Ἑν τὸ πᾶν, as unity and multiplicity at once. The idea that the simultaneous points in the causal chains, or meridians, represent meaningful coincidences would only hold water if the first cause really were a unity. But if it were a multiplicity, which is just as likely, then Schopenhauer's whole explanation collapses, quite apart from the fact, which we have only recently realized, that natural law possesses a merely statistical validity and thus keeps the door open to indeterminism. Neither philosophical reflection nor experience can provide any evidence for the regular occurrence of these two kinds of connection, in which the same thing is both subject and object. Schopenhauer thought and wrote at a time when causality held sovereign sway as a category *a priori* and had therefore to be dragged in to explain meaningful coincidences. But, as we have seen, it can do this with some degree of probability only if we have recourse to the

16 P. 45. [Irvine, pp. 49f.]
17 P. 46. [Irvine, p. 50.]
18 Hence my term "synchronicity."

other, equally arbitrary assumption of the unity of the first cause. It then follows as a *necessity* that every point on a given meridian stands in a relationship of meaningful coincidence to every other point on the same degree of latitude. This conclusion, however, goes far beyond the bounds of what is empirically possible, for it credits meaningful coincidences with occurring so regularly and systematically that their verification would be either unnecessary or the simplest thing in the world. Schopenhauer's examples carry as much or as little conviction as all the others. Nevertheless, it is to his credit that he saw the problem and understood that there are no facile *ad hoc* explanations. Since this problem is concerned with the foundations of our epistemology, he derived it in accordance with the general trend of his philosophy from a transcendental premise, from the Will which creates life and being on all levels, and which modulates each of these levels in such a way that they are not only in harmony with their synchronous parallels but also prepare and arrange future events in the form of Fate or Providence.

829   In contrast to Schopenhauer's accustomed pessimism, this utterance has an almost friendly and optimistic tone which we can hardly sympathize with today. One of the most problematical and momentous centuries the world has ever known separates us from that still medievalistic age when the philosophizing mind believed it could make assertions beyond what could be empirically proved. It was an age of large views, which did not cry halt and think that the limits of nature had been reached just where the scientific road-builders had come to a temporary stop. Thus Schopenhauer, with true philosophical vision, opened up a field for reflection whose peculiar phenomenology he was not equipped to understand, though he outlined it more or less correctly. He recognized that with their *omina* and *praesagia* astrology and the various intuitive methods of interpreting fate have a common denominator which he sought to discover by means of "transcendental speculation." He recognized, equally rightly, that it was a problem of principle of the first order, unlike all those before and after him who operated with futile conceptions of some kind of energy transmission, or conveniently dismissed the whole thing as nonsense in order to

13

avoid a too difficult task.[19] Schopenhauer's attempt is the more remarkable in that it was made at a time when the tremendous advance of the natural sciences had convinced everybody that causality alone could be considered the final principle of explanation. Instead of ignoring all those experiences which refuse to bow down to the sovereign rule of causality, he tried, as we have seen, to fit them into his deterministic view of the world. In so doing, he forced concepts like prefiguration, correspondence, and pre-established harmony, which as a universal order coexisting with the causal one have always underlain man's explanations of nature, into the causal scheme, probably because he felt—and rightly—that the scientific view of the world based on natural law, though he did not doubt its validity, nevertheless lacked something which played a considerable role in the classical and medieval view (as it also does in the intuitive feelings of modern man).

830   The mass of facts collected by Gurney, Myers, and Podmore [20] inspired three other investigators—Dariex,[21] Richet,[22] and Flammarion [23]— to tackle the problem in terms of a probability calculus. Dariex found a probability of 1 : 4,114,545 for telepathic precognitions of death, which means that the explanation of such a warning as due to "chance" is more than four million times more improbable than explaining it as a "telepathic," or acausal, meaningful coincidence. The astronomer Flammarion reckoned a probability of no less than 1 : 804,622,222 for a particularly well-observed instance of "phantasms of the living." [24] He was also the first to link up other suspicious happenings with the general interest in phenomena connected with death. Thus he relates [25] that, while writing his book on the atmosphere, he was just at the chapter on wind-force when a sudden gust of wind swept all his papers off the table and blew them out of the window. He also cites, as an example of triple coincidence, the edifying story of

[19] Here I must make an exception of Kant, whose treatise *Dreams of a Spirit-Seer, Illustrated by Dreams of Metaphysics* pointed the way for Schopenhauer.
[20] Edmund Gurney, Frederic W. H. Myers, and Frank Podmore, *Phantasms of the Living.*   [21] Xavier Dariex, "Le Hazard et la télépathie."
[22] Charles Richet, "Relations de diverses expériences sur transmission mentale, la lucidité, et autres phénomènes non explicable par les données scientifiques actuelles."   [23] Camille Flammarion, *The Unknown*, pp. 191ff.
[24] Ibid., p. 202.   [25] Pp. 192f.

Monsieur de Fortgibu and the plum-pudding.[26] The fact that he mentions these coincidences at all in connection with the problem of telepathy shows that Flammarion had a distinct intuition, albeit an unconscious one, of a far more comprehensive principle.

831   The writer Wilhelm von Scholz [27] has collected a number of stories showing the strange ways in which lost or stolen objects come back to their owners. Among other things, he tells the story of a mother who took a photograph of her small son in the Black Forest. She left the film to be developed in Strassburg. But, owing to the outbreak of war, she was unable to fetch it and gave it up for lost. In 1916 she bought a film in Frankfurt in order to take a photograph of her daughter, who had been born in the meantime. When the film was developed it was found to be doubly exposed: the picture underneath was the photograph she had taken of her son in 1914! The old film had not been developed and had somehow got into circulation again among the new films. The author comes to the understandable conclusion that everything points to the "mutual attraction of related objects," or an "elective affinity." He suspects that these happenings are arranged as if they were the dream of a "greater and more comprehensive consciousness, which is unknowable."

832   The problem of chance has been approached from the psychological angle by Herbert Silberer.[28] He shows that apparently meaningful coincidences are partly unconscious arrangements, and partly unconscious, arbitrary interpretations. He takes no account either of parapsychic phenomena or of synchronicity, and theoretically he does not go much beyond the causalism of Schopenhauer. Apart from its valuable psychological criticism of our methods of evaluating chance, Silberer's

---

26 Pp. 194ff. A certain M. Deschamps, when a boy in Orléans, was once given a piece of plum-pudding by a M. de Fortgibu. Ten years later he discovered another plum-pudding in a Paris restaurant, and asked if he could have a piece. It turned out, however, that the plum-pudding was already ordered—by M. de Fortgibu. Many years afterwards M. Deschamps was invited to partake of a plum-pudding as a special rarity. While he was eating it he remarked that the only thing lacking was M. de Fortgibu. At that moment the door opened and an old, old man in the last stages of disorientation walked in: M. de Fortgibu, who had got hold of the wrong address and burst in on the party by mistake.

27 *Der Zufall: Eine Vorform des Schicksals.*

28 *Der Zufall und die Koboldstreiche des Unbewussten.*

study contains no reference to the occurrence of meaningful coincidences as here understood.

833   Decisive evidence for the existence of acausal combinations of events has been furnished, with adequate scientific safeguards, only very recently, mainly through the experiments of J. B. Rhine and his fellow-workers,[29] who have not, however, recognized the far-reaching conclusions that must be drawn from their findings. Up to the present no critical argument that cannot be refuted has been brought against these experiments. The experiment consists, in principle, in an experimenter turning up, one after another, a series of numbered cards bearing simple geometrical patterns. At the same time the subject, separated by a screen from the experimenter, is given the task of guessing the signs as they are turned up. A pack of twenty-five cards is used, each five of which carry the same sign. Five cards are marked with a star, five with a square, five with a circle, five with wavy lines, and five with a cross. The experimenter naturally does not know the order in which the pack is arranged, nor has the subject any opportunity of seeing the cards. Many of the experiments were negative, since the result did not exceed the probability of five chance hits. In the case of certain subjects, however, some results were distinctly above probability. The first series of experiments consisted in each subject trying to guess the cards 800 times. The average result showed 6.5 hits for 25 cards, which is 1.5 more than the chance probability of 5 hits. The probability of there being a chance deviation of 1.5 from the number 5 works out at 1 : 250,000. This proportion shows that the probability of a chance deviation is not exactly high, since it is to be expected only once in 250,000 cases. The results vary according to the specific gift of the individual subject. One young man, who in numerous experiments scored an average of 10 hits for every 25 cards (double the probable number), once guessed all 25 cards correctly, which

---

[29] J. B. Rhine, *Extra-Sensory Perception* and *New Frontiers of the Mind*. J. G. Pratt, J. B. Rhine, C. E. Stuart, B. M. Smith, and J. A. Greenwood, *Extra-Sensory Perception after Sixty Years*. A general survey of the findings in Rhine, *The Reach of the Mind*, and also in the valuable book by G. N. M. Tyrrell, *The Personality of Man*. A short résumé in Rhine, "An Introduction to the Work of Extra-Sensory Perception." S. G. Soal and F. Bateman, *Modern Experiments in Telepathy*.

gives a probability of 1 : 298,023,223,876,953,125. The possibility of the pack being shuffled in some arbitrary way is guarded against by an apparatus which shuffles the cards automatically, independently of the experimenter.

834   After the first series of experiments the spatial distance between the experimenter and the subject was increased, in one case to 250 miles. The average result of numerous experiments amounted here to 10.1 hits for 25 cards. In another series of experiments, when experimenter and subject were in the same room, the score was 11.4 for 25; when the subject was in the next room, 9.7 for 25; when two rooms away, 12.0 for 25. Rhine mentions the experiments of F. L. Usher and E. L. Burt, which were conducted with positive results over a distance of 960 miles.[30] With the aid of synchronized watches experiments were also conducted between Durham, North Carolina, and Zagreb, Yugoslavia, about 4,000 miles, with equally positive results.[31]

835   The fact that distance has no effect in principle shows that the thing in question cannot be a phenomenon of force or energy, for otherwise the distance to be overcome and the diffusion in space would cause a diminution of the effect, and it is more than probable that the score would fall proportionately to the square of the distance. Since this is obviously not the case, we have no alternative but to assume that distance is psychically variable, and may in certain circumstances be reduced to vanishing point by a psychic condition.

836   Even more remarkable is the fact that *time* is not in principle a prohibiting factor either; that is to say, the scanning of a series of cards to be turned up in the future produces a score that exceeds chance probability. The results of Rhine's time experiment show a probability of 1 : 400,000, which means a considerable probability of there being some factor independent of time. They point, in other words, to a psychic relativity of time, since the experiment was concerned with perceptions of events which had not yet occurred. In these circumstances the time factor seems to have been eliminated by a psychic function or psychic condition which is also capable of abolishing the spatial factor. If, in the spatial experiments, we were obliged to admit that energy does not decrease with distance, then the

30 *The Reach of the Mind* (1954 edn.), p. 48.
31 Rhine and Betty M. Humphrey, "A Transoceanic ESP Experiment."

time experiments make it completely impossible for us even to think of there being any energy relationship between the perception and the future event. We must give up at the outset all explanations in terms of energy, which amounts to saying that events of this kind cannot be considered from the point of view of causality, for causality presupposes the existence of space and time in so far as all observations are ultimately based upon bodies in motion.

837   Among Rhine's experiments we must also mention the experiments with dice. The subject has the task of throwing the dice (which is done by an apparatus), and at the same time he has to wish that one number (say 3) will turn up as many times as possible. The results of this so-called PK (psychokinetic) experiment were positive, the more so the more dice were used at one time.[32] If space and time prove to be psychically relative, then the moving body must possess, or be subject to, a corresponding relativity.

838   One consistent experience in all these experiments is the fact that the number of hits scored tends to sink after the first attempt, and the results then become negative. But if, for some inner or outer reason, there is a freshening of interest on the subject's part, the score rises again. Lack of interest and boredom are negative factors; enthusiasm, positive expectation, hope, and belief in the possibility of ESP make for good results and seem to be the real conditions which determine whether there are going to be any results at all. In this connection it is interesting to note that the well-known English medium, Mrs. Eileen J. Garrett, achieved bad results in the Rhine experiments because, as she herself admits, she was unable to summon up any feeling for the "soulless" test-cards.

839   These few hints may suffice to give the reader at least a superficial idea of these experiments. The above-mentioned book by G. N. M. Tyrrell, late president of the Society for Psychical Research, contains an excellent summing-up of all experiences in this field. Its author himself rendered great service to ESP research. From the physicist's side the ESP experiments have been evaluated in a positive sense by Robert A.

[32] *The Reach of the Mind*, pp. 75ff.

McConnell in an article entitled "ESP—Fact or Fancy?" [33]

840   As is only to be expected, every conceivable kind of attempt has been made to explain away these results, which seem to border on the miraculous and frankly impossible. But all such attempts come to grief on the facts, and the facts refuse so far to be argued out of existence. Rhine's experiments confront us with the fact that there are events which are related to one another experimentally, and in this case *meaningfully*, without there being any possibility of proving that this relation is a causal one, since the "transmission" exhibits none of the known properties of energy. There is therefore good reason to doubt whether it is a question of transmission at all. The time experiments rule out any such thing in principle, for it would be absurd to suppose that a situation which does not yet exist and will only occur in the future could transmit itself as a phenomenon of energy to a receiver in the present.[34] It seems more likely that scientific explanation will have to begin with a criticism of our concepts of space and time on the one hand, and with the unconscious on the other. As I have said, it is impossible, with our present resources, to explain ESP, or the fact of meaningful coincidence, as a phenomenon of energy. This makes an end of the causal explanation as well, for "effect" cannot be understood as anything except a phenomenon of energy. Therefore it cannot be a question of cause and effect, but of a falling together in time, a kind of simultaneity. Because of this quality of simultaneity, I have picked on the term "synchronicity" to designate a hypothetical factor equal in rank to causality as a principle of explanation. In my essay "On the Nature of the Psyche," [35] I considered synchronicity as a psychically conditioned relativity of space and time. Rhine's experiments show that in relation to the psyche space and time are, so to speak, "elastic" and can apparently be reduced almost to vanishing point, as though they were dependent on psychic conditions and did not exist in themselves but were only "postulated" by the conscious mind. In man's original view of the world, as we

[33] Professor Pauli was kind enough to draw my attention to this paper, which appeared in 1949.
[34] Kammerer has dealt, not altogether convincingly, with the question of the "countereffect of the succeeding state on the preceding one" (cf. *Das Gesetz der Serie*, pp. 131f.).   [35] Cf. above, par. 440.

find it among primitives, space and time have a very precarious existence. They become "fixed" concepts only in the course of his mental development, thanks largely to the introduction of measurement. In themselves, space and time consist of *nothing*. They are hypostatized concepts born of the discriminating activity of the conscious mind, and they form the indispensable co-ordinates for describing the behaviour of bodies in motion. They are, therefore, essentially psychic in origin, which is probably the reason that impelled Kant to regard them as *a priori* categories. But if space and time are only apparently properties of bodies in motion and are created by the intellectual needs of the observer, then their relativization by psychic conditions is no longer a matter for astonishment but is brought within the bounds of possibility. This possibility presents itself when the psyche observes, not external bodies, but *itself*. That is precisely what happens in Rhine's experiments: the subject's answer is not the result of his observing the physical cards, it is a product of pure imagination, of "chance" ideas which reveal the structure of that which produces them, namely the unconscious. Here I will only point out that it is the decisive factors in the unconscious psyche, the archetypes, which constitute the structure of the collective unconscious. The latter represents a psyche that is identical in all individuals. It cannot be directly perceived or "represented," in contrast to the perceptible psychic phenomena, and on account of its "irrepresentable" nature I have called it "psychoid."

841   The archetypes are formal factors responsible for the organization of unconscious psychic processes: they are "patterns of behaviour." At the same time they have a "specific charge" and develop numinous effects which express themselves as *affects*. The affect produces a partial *abaissement du niveau mental,* for although it raises a particular content to a supernormal degree of luminosity, it does so by withdrawing so much energy from other possible contents of consciousness that they become darkened and eventually unconscious. Owing to the restriction of consciousness produced by the affect so long as it lasts, there is a corresponding lowering of orientation which in its turn gives the unconscious a favourable opportunity to slip into the space vacated. Thus we regularly find that unexpected or otherwise inhibited unconscious contents break through and find expres-

sion in the affect. Such contents are very often of an inferior or primitive nature and thus betray their archetypal origin. As I shall show further on, certain phenomena of simultaneity or synchronicity seem to be bound up with the archetypes. That is the reason why I mention the archetypes here.

842   The extraordinary spatial orientation of animals may also point to the psychic relativity of space and time. The puzzling time-orientation of the palolo worm, for instance, whose tail-segments, loaded with sexual products, always appear on the surface of the sea the day before the last quarter of the moon in October and November,[36] might be mentioned in this con-nection. One of the causes suggested is the acceleration of the earth owing to the gravitational pull of the moon at this time. But, for astronomical reasons, this explanation cannot possibly be right.[37] The relation which undoubtedly exists between the human menstruation period and the course of the moon is connected with the latter only numerically and does not really coincide with it. Nor has it been proved that it ever did.

*

843   The problem of synchronicity has puzzled me for a long time, ever since the middle twenties,[38] when I was investigating the phenomena of the collective unconscious and kept on com-ing across connections which I simply could not explain as chance groupings or "runs." What I found were "coincidences" which were connected so meaningfully that their "chance" concurrence would represent a degree of improbability that would have to be expressed by an astronomical figure. By way

36 To be more accurate, the swarming begins a little before and ends a little after this day, when the swarming is at its height. The months vary according to location. The palolo worm, or wawo, of Amboina is said to appear at full moon in March. (A. F. Krämer, Über den Bau der Korallenriffe.)

37 Fritz Dahns, "Das Schwärmen des Palolo."

38 Even before that time certain doubts had arisen in me as to the unlimited applicability of the causal principle in psychology. In the foreword to the 1st edn. of Collected Papers on Analytical Psychology, I had written (p. ix): "Causality is only one principle and psychology essentially cannot be exhausted by causal methods only, because the mind [= psyche] lives by aims as well." Psychic finality rests on a "pre-existent" meaning which becomes problematical only when it is an unconscious arrangement. In that case we have to suppose a "knowledge" prior to all consciousness. Hans Driesch comes to the same conclusion (Die "Seele" als elementarer Naturfaktor, pp. 80ff.).

of example, I shall mention an incident from my own observation. A young woman I was treating had, at a critical moment, a dream in which she was given a golden scarab. While she was telling me this dream I sat with my back to the closed window. Suddenly I heard a noise behind me, like a gentle tapping. I turned round and saw a flying insect knocking against the window-pane from outside. I opened the window and caught the creature in the air as it flew in. It was the nearest analogy to a golden scarab that one finds in our latitudes, a scarabaeid beetle, the common rose-chafer (*Cetonia aurata*), which contrary to its usual habits had evidently felt an urge to get into a dark room at this particular moment. I must admit that nothing like it ever happened to me before or since, and that the dream of the patient has remained unique in my experience.[38a]

844 I should like to mention another case that is typical of a certain category of events. The wife of one of my patients, a man in his fifties, once told me in conversation that, at the deaths of her mother and her grandmother, a number of birds gathered outside the windows of the death-chamber. I had heard similar stories from other people. When her husband's treatment was nearing its end, his neurosis having been cleared up, he developed some apparently quite innocuous symptoms which seemed to me, however, to be those of heart-disease. I sent him along to a specialist, who after examining him told me in writing that he could find no cause for anxiety. On the way back from this consultation (with the medical report in his pocket) my patient collapsed in the street. As he was brought home dying, his wife was already in a great state of anxiety because, soon after her husband had gone to the doctor, a whole flock of birds alighted on their house. She naturally remembered the similar incidents that had happened at the death of her own relatives, and feared the worst.

845 Although I was personally acquainted with the people concerned and know very well that the facts here reported are true, I do not imagine for a moment that this will induce anybody who is determined to regard such things as pure "chance" to change his mind. My sole object in relating these two incidents

---

[38a] [The case is discussed more fully below, par. 982.—EDITORS.]

is simply to give some indication of how meaningful coincidences usually present themselves in practical life. The meaningful connection is obvious enough in the first case in view of the approximate identity of the chief objects (the scarab and the beetle); but in the second case the death and the flock of birds seem to be incommensurable with one another. If one considers, however, that in the Babylonian Hades the souls wore a "feather dress," and that in ancient Egypt the *ba*, or soul, was thought of as a bird,[39] it is not too far-fetched to suppose that there may be some archetypal symbolism at work. Had such an incident occurred in a dream, that interpretation would be justified by the comparative psychological material. There also seems to be an archetypal foundation to the first case. It was an extraordinarily difficult case to treat, and up to the time of the dream little or no progress had been made. I should explain that the main reason for this was my patient's animus, which was steeped in Cartesian philosophy and clung so rigidly to its own idea of reality that the efforts of three doctors—I was the third—had not been able to weaken it. Evidently something quite irrational was needed which was beyond my powers to produce. The dream alone was enough to disturb ever so slightly the rationalistic attitude of my patient. But when the "scarab" came flying in through the window in actual fact, her natural being could burst through the armour of her animus possession and the process of transformation could at last begin to move. Any essential change of attitude signifies a psychic renewal which is usually accompanied by symbols of rebirth in the patient's dreams and fantasies. The scarab is a classic example of a rebirth symbol. The ancient Egyptian Book of What Is in the Netherworld describes how the dead sun-god changes himself at the tenth station into Khepri, the scarab, and then, at the twelfth station, mounts the barge which carries the rejuvenated sun-god into the morning sky. The only difficulty here is that with educated people cryptomnesia often cannot be ruled out with certainty (although my patient did not happen to know this symbol). But this does not alter the fact that the psychologist is continually coming up against cases where the emergence of

---

[39] In Homer the souls of the dead "twitter." [*Odyssey*, Book XI.—EDITORS.]

symbolic parallels [40] cannot be explained without the hypothesis of the collective unconscious.

846   Meaningful coincidences—which are to be distinguished from meaningless chance groupings [41]—therefore seem to rest on an archetypal foundation. At least all the cases in my experience —and there is a large number of them—show this characteristic. What that means I have already indicated above.[42] Although anyone with my experience in this field can easily recognize their archetypal character, he will find it difficult to link them up with the psychic conditions in Rhine's experiments, because the latter contain no direct evidence of any constellation of the archetype. Nor is the emotional situation the same as in my examples. Nevertheless, it must be remembered that with Rhine the first series of experiments generally produced the best results, which then quickly fell off. But when it was possible to arouse a new interest in the essentially rather boring experiment, the results improved again. It follows from this that the emotional factor plays an important role. Affectivity, however, rests to a large extent on the instincts, whose formal aspect is the archetype.

847   There is yet another psychological analogy between my two cases and the Rhine experiments, though it is not quite so obvious. These apparently quite different situations have as their common characteristic an element of "impossibility." The patient with the scarab found herself in an "impossible" situation because the treatment had got stuck and there seemed to be no way out of the impasse. In such situations, if they are serious enough, archetypal dreams are likely to occur which point out a possible line of advance one would never have thought of oneself. It is this kind of situation that constellates the archetype with the greatest regularity. In certain cases the psychotherapist therefore sees himself obliged to discover the

40 Naturally these can only be verified when the doctor himself has the necessary knowledge of symbology.

41 [Statistical analysis is designed to separate out groupings (termed dispersions) due to random activity from significant dispersions in which causes may be looked for. On Professor Jung's hypothesis, however, dispersions due to chance can be subdivided into meaningful and meaningless. The meaningless dispersions due to chance are made meaningful by the activation of the psychoid archetype.— Editors.]

42 Cf. par. 841; also "On the Nature of the Psyche," par. 404f.

rationally insoluble problem towards which the patient's unconscious is steering. Once this is found, the deeper layers of the unconscious, the primordial images, are activated and the transformation of the personality can get under way.

348 In the second case there was the half-unconscious fear and the threat of a lethal end with no possibility of an adequate recognition of the situation. In Rhine's experiment it is the "impossibility" of the task that ultimately fixes the subject's attention on the processes going on inside him, and thus gives the unconscious a chance to manifest itself. The questions set by the ESP experiment have an emotional effect right from the start, since they postulate something unknowable as being potentially knowable and in that way take the possibility of a miracle seriously into account. This, regardless of the subject's scepticism, immediately appeals to his unconscious readiness to witness a miracle, and to the hope, latent in all men, that such a thing may yet be possible. Primitive superstition lies just below the surface of even the most toughminded individuals, and it is precisely those who most fight against it who are the first to succumb to its suggestive effects. When therefore a serious experiment with all the authority of science behind it touches this readiness, it will inevitably give rise to an emotion which either accepts or rejects it with a good deal of affectivity. At all events an affective expectation is present in one form or another even though it may be denied.

349 Here I would like to call attention to a possible misunderstanding which may be occasioned by the term "synchronicity." I chose this term because the simultaneous occurrence of two meaningfully but not causally connected events seemed to me an essential criterion. I am therefore using the general concept of synchronicity in the special sense of a coincidence in time of two or more causally unrelated events which have the same or a similar meaning, in contrast to "synchronism," which simply means the simultaneous occurrence of two events.

350 Synchronicity therefore means the simultaneous occurrence of a certain psychic state with one or more external events which appear as meaningful parallels to the momentary subjective state—and, in certain cases, vice versa. My two examples illustrate this in different ways. In the case of the scarab the simultaneity is immediately obvious, but not in the second

25

example. It is true that the flock of birds occasioned a vague fear, but that can be explained causally. The wife of my patient was certainly not conscious beforehand of any fear that could be compared with my own apprehensions, for the symptoms (pains in the throat) were not of a kind to make the layman suspect anything bad. The unconscious, however, often knows more than the conscious, and it seems to me possible that the woman's unconscious had already got wind of the danger. If, therefore, we rule out a conscious psychic content such as the idea of deadly danger, there is an obvious simultaneity between the flock of birds, in its traditional meaning, and the death of the husband. The psychic state, if we disregard the possible but still not demonstrable excitation of the unconscious, appears to be dependent on the external event. The woman's psyche is nevertheless involved in so far as the birds settled on her house and were observed by her. For this reason it seems to me probable that her unconscious was in fact constellated. The flock of birds has, as such, a traditional mantic significance.[43] This is also apparent in the woman's own interpretation, and it therefore looks as if the birds represented an unconscious premonition of death. The physicians of the Romantic Age would probably have talked of "sympathy" or "magnetism." But, as I have said, such phenomena cannot be explained causally unless one permits oneself the most fantastic *ad hoc* hypotheses.

851   The interpretation of the birds as an omen is, as we have seen, based on two earlier coincidences of a similar kind. It did not yet exist at the time of the grandmother's death. There the coincidence was represented only by the death and the gathering of the birds. Both then and at the mother's death the coincidence was obvious, but in the third case it could only be verified when the dying man was brought into the house.

852   I mention these complications because they have an important bearing on the concept of synchronicity. Let us take another

---

43 A literary example is "The Cranes of Ibycus." [A poem by Schiller (1798), inspired by the story of the Greek poet murdered by robbers who were brought to justice through the appearance of a swarm of cranes. As cranes had also flown over the scene of the crime, the murderers cried out at the sight and so betrayed themselves.—EDITORS.] Similarly, when a flock of chattering magpies settles on a house it is supposed to mean death, and so on. Cf. also the significance of auguries.

example: An acquaintance of mine saw and experienced in a dream the sudden death of a friend, with all the characteristic details. The dreamer was in Europe at the time and the friend in America. The death was confirmed next morning by telegram, and ten days later a letter confirmed the details. Comparison of European time with American time showed that the death occurred at least an hour before the dream. The dreamer had gone to bed late and not slept until about one o'clock. The dream occurred at approximately two in the morning. The dream experience is *not synchronous* with the death. Experiences of this kind frequently take place a little before or after the critical event. J. W. Dunne [44] mentions a particularly instructive dream he had in the spring of 1902, when serving in the Boer War. He seemed to be standing on a volcanic mountain. It was an island, which he had dreamed about before and knew was threatened by a catastrophic volcanic eruption (like Krakatoa). Terrified, he wanted to save the four thousand inhabitants. He tried to get the French officials on the neighbouring island to mobilize all available shipping for the rescue work. Here the dream began to develop the typical nightmare motifs of hurrying, chasing, and not arriving on time, and all the while there hovered before his mind the words: "Four thousand people will be killed unless——" A few days later Dunne received with his mail a copy of the *Daily Telegraph,* and his eye fell on the following headlines:

VOLCANO DISASTER
IN MARTINIQUE

———

Town Swept Away

———

AN AVALANCHE OF FLAME

———

*Probable Loss of Over
40,000 Lives*

853   The dream did not take place at the moment of the actual catastrophe, but only when the paper was already on its way to

44 *An Experiment with Time* (2nd edn.), pp. 34ff.

him with the news. While reading it, he misread 40,000 as 4,000. The mistake became fixed as a paramnesia, so that whenever he told the dream he invariably said 4,000 instead of 40,000. Not until fifteen years later, when he copied out the article, did he discover his mistake. His unconscious knowledge had made the same mistake in reading as himself.

854 The fact that he dreamed this shortly before the news reached him is something that happens fairly frequently. We often dream about people from whom we receive a letter by the next post. I have ascertained on several occasions that at the moment when the dream occurred the letter was already lying in the post-office of the addressee. I can also confirm, from my own experience, the reading mistake. During the Christmas of 1918 I was much occupied with Orphism, and in particular with the Orphic fragment in Malalas, where the Primordial Light is described as the "trinitarian Metis, Phanes, Erice-paeus." I consistently read Erica*paeus* instead of Erice*paeus*, as in the text. (Actually both readings occur.) This misreading became fixed as a paramnesia, and later I always remembered the name as Ericapaeus and only discovered thirty years afterward that Malalas' text has Ericepaeus. Just at this time one of my patients, whom I had not seen for a month and who knew nothing of my studies, had a dream in which an unknown man handed her a piece of paper, and on it was written a "Latin" hymn to a god called *Ericipaeus*. The dreamer was able to write this hymn down upon waking. The language it was written in was a peculiar mixture of Latin, French, and Italian. The lady had an elementary knowledge of Latin, knew a bit more Italian, and spoke French fluently. The name "Ericipaeus" was completely unknown to her, which is not surprising as she had no knowledge of the classics. Our two towns were about fifty miles apart, and there had been no communication between us for a month. Oddly enough, the variant of the name affected the very same vowel which I too had misread (*a* instead of *e*), but her unconscious misread it another way (*i* instead of *e*). I can only suppose that she unconsciously "read" not my mistake but the text in which the Latin transliteration "Ericepaeus" occurs, and was evidently put off her stroke by my misreading.

855 Synchronistic events rest on the *simultaneous occurrence of two different psychic states*. One of them is the normal, probable

28

state (i.e., the one that is causally explicable), and the other, the critical experience, is the one that cannot be derived causally from the first. In the case of sudden death the critical experience cannot be recognized immediately as "extra-sensory perception" but can only be verified as such afterwards. Yet even in the case of the "scarab" what is immediately experienced is a psychic state or psychic image which differs from the dream image only because it can be verified immediately. In the case of the flock of birds there was in the woman an unconscious excitation or fear which was certainly conscious *to me* and caused me to send the patient to a heart specialist. In all these cases, whether it is a question of spatial or of temporal ESP, we find a simultaneity of the normal or ordinary state with another state or experience which is not causally derivable from it, and whose objective existence can only be verified afterwards. This definition must be borne in mind particularly when it is a question of future events. They are evidently not *synchronous* but are *synchronistic,* since they are experienced as psychic images *in the present,* as though the objective event already existed. An unexpected content which is directly or indirectly connected with some objective external event coincides with the ordinary psychic state: this is what I call synchronicity, and I maintain that we are dealing with exactly the same category of events whether their objectivity appears separated from my consciousness in space or in time. This view is confirmed by Rhine's results in so far as they were not influenced by changes in space or time. Space and time, the conceptual co-ordinates of bodies in motion, are probably at bottom one and the same (which is why we speak of a long or short "space of time"), and Philo Judaeus said long ago that "the extension of heavenly motion is time." [45] Synchronicity in space can equally well be conceived as perception in time, but remarkably enough it is not so easy to understand synchronicity in time as spatial, for we cannot imagine any space in which future events are objectively present and could be experienced as such through a reduction of this spatial distance. But since experience has shown that under certain conditions space and time can be reduced almost to zero, causality disappears along with them, because causality is bound up with

[45] *De opificio mundi,* 26. ("Διάστημα τῆς τοῦ οὐρανοῦ κινήσεώς ἐστι ὁ χρόνος.")

the existence of space and time and physical changes, and consists essentially in the succession of cause and effect. For this reason synchronistic phenomena cannot in principle be associated with any conceptions of causality. Hence the interconnection of meaningfully coincident factors must necessarily be thought of as acausal.

856   Here, for want of a demonstrable cause, we are all too likely to fall into the temptation of positing a *transcendental* one. But a "cause" can only be a demonstrable quantity. A "transcendental cause" is a contradiction in terms, because anything transcendental cannot by definition be demonstrated. If we don't want to risk the hypothesis of acausality, then the only alternative is to explain synchronistic phenomena as mere chance, which brings us into conflict with Rhine's ESP discoveries and other well-attested facts reported in the literature of parapsychology. Or else we are driven to the kind of reflections I described above, and must subject our basic principles of explanation to the criticism that space and time are constants in any given system only when they are measured without regard to psychic conditions. That is what regularly happens in scientific experiments. But when an event is observed without experimental restrictions, the observer can easily be influenced by an emotional state which alters space and time by "contraction." Every emotional state produces an alteration of consciousness which Janet called *abaissement du niveau mental;* that is to say there is a certain narrowing of consciousness and a corresponding strengthening of the unconscious which, particularly in the case of strong affects, is noticeable even to the layman. The tone of the unconscious is heightened, thereby creating a gradient for the unconscious to flow towards the conscious. The conscious then comes under the influence of unconscious instinctual impulses and contents. These are as a rule complexes whose ultimate basis is the archetype, the "instinctual pattern." The unconscious also contains subliminal perceptions (as well as forgotten memory-images that cannot be reproduced at the moment, and perhaps not at all). Among the subliminal contents we must distinguish perceptions from what I would call an inexplicable "knowledge," or an "immediacy" of psychic images. Whereas the sense-perceptions can be related to probable or possible sensory stimuli below the threshold of con-

sciousness, this "knowledge," or the "immediacy" of unconscious images, either has no recognizable foundation, or else we find that there are recognizable causal connections with certain already existing, and often archetypal, contents. But these images, whether rooted in an already existing basis or not, stand in an analogous or equivalent (i.e., meaningful) relationship to objective occurrences which have no recognizable or even conceivable causal relationship with them. How could an event remote in space and time produce a corresponding psychic image when the transmission of energy necessary for this is not even thinkable? However incomprehensible it may appear, we are finally compelled to assume that there is in the unconscious something like an *a priori* knowledge or an "immediacy" of events which lacks any causal basis. At any rate our conception of causality is incapable of explaining the facts.

857

In view of this complicated situation it may be worth while to recapitulate the argument discussed above, and this can best be done with the aid of our examples. In Rhine's experiment I made the assumption that, owing to the tense expectation or emotional state of the subject, an already existing, correct, but unconscious image of the result enables his conscious mind to score a more than chance number of hits. The scarab dream is a conscious representation arising from an unconscious, already existing image of the situation that will occur on the following day, i.e., the recounting of the dream and the appearance of the rose-chafer. The wife of the patient who died had an unconscious knowledge of the impending death. The flock of birds evoked the corresponding memory-images and consequently her fear. Similarly, the almost simultaneous dream of the violent death of the friend arose from an already existing unconscious knowledge of it.

858

In all these cases and others like them there seems to be an *a priori*, causally inexplicable knowledge of a situation which at the time is unknowable. Synchronicity therefore consists of two factors: *a*) An unconscious image comes into consciousness either directly (i.e., literally) or indirectly (symbolized or suggested) in the form of a dream, idea, or premonition. *b*) An objective situation coincides with this content. The one is as puzzling as the other. How does the unconscious image arise, and how the coincidence? I understand only too well why peo-

31

ple prefer to doubt the reality of these things. Here I will only pose the question. Later in this study I will try to answer it.

859   As regards the role which affects play in the occurrence of synchronistic events, I should perhaps mention that this is by no means a new idea but was already known to Avicenna and Albertus Magnus. On the subject of magic, Albertus Magnus writes:

I discovered an instructive account [of magic] in Avicenna's *Liber sextus naturalium*, which says that a certain power [46] to alter things indwells in the human soul and subordinates the other things to her, particularly when she is swept into a great excess of love or hate or the like.[47] When therefore the soul of a man falls into a great excess of any passion, it can be proved by experiment that it [the excess] binds things [magically] and alters them in the way it wants,[48] and for a long time I did not believe it, but after I had read the nigromantic books and others of the kind on signs and magic, I found that the emotionality [49] of the human soul is the chief cause of all these things, whether because, on account of her great emotion, she alters her bodily substance and the other things towards which she strives, or because, on account of her dignity, the other, lower things are subject to her, or because the appropriate hour or astrological situation or another power coincides with so inordinate an emotion, and we [in consequence] believe that what this power does is then done by the soul.[50] . . . Whoever would learn the secret of doing and undoing these things must know that everyone can influence everything magically if he falls into a great excess . . . and he must do it at that hour when the excess befalls him, and operate with the things which the soul prescribes. For the soul is then so desirous of the matter she would accomplish that of her own accord she seizes on the more significant and better astrological hour which also rules over the things suited to that matter. . . . Thus it is the soul who desires a thing more intensely, who makes things more effective and more like what comes forth. . . . Such is the manner of production with everything the soul intensely desires. Everything she does with that aim in view possesses motive power and efficacy for what the soul desires.[51]

[46] "virtus"
[47] "quando ipsa fertur in magnum amoris excessum aut odii aut alicuius talium."
[48] "fertur in grandem excessum alicuius passionis invenitur experimento manifesto quod ipse ligat res et alterat ad idem quod desiderat"   [49] "affectio"
[50] "cum tali affectione exterminata concurrat hora conveniens aut ordo coelestis aut alia virtus, quae quodvis faciet, illud reputavimus tunc animam facere."
[51] *De mirabilibus mundi* (1485?).

860   This text shows clearly that synchronistic ("magical") happenings are regarded as being dependent on affects. Naturally
Albertus Magnus, in accordance with the spirit of his age, explains this by postulating a magical faculty in the soul, without
considering that the psychic process itself is just as much "arranged" as the coinciding image which anticipates the external
physical process. This image originates in the unconscious and
therefore belongs to those "cogitationes quae sunt a nobis
independentes," which, in the opinion of Arnold Geulincx, are
prompted by God and do not spring from our own thinking.[52]
Goethe thinks of synchronistic events in the same "magical"
way. Thus he says, in his conversations with Eckermann: "We
all have certain electric and magnetic powers within us and
ourselves exercise an attractive and repelling force, according as
we come into touch with something like or unlike." [53]

861   After these general considerations let us return to the problem of the empirical basis of synchronicity. The main difficulty
here is to procure empirical material from which we can draw
reasonably certain conclusions, and unfortunately this difficulty
is not an easy one to solve. The experiences in question are not
ready to hand. We must therefore look in the obscurest corners
and summon up courage to shock the prejudices of our age if
we want to broaden the basis of our understanding of nature.
When Galileo discovered the moons of Jupiter with his telescope he immediately came into head-on collision with the
prejudices of his learned contemporaries. Nobody knew what
a telescope was and what it could do. Never before had anyone
talked of the moons of Jupiter. Naturally every age thinks that
all ages before it were prejudiced, and today we think this more
than ever and are just as wrong as all previous ages that thought
so. How often have we not seen the truth condemned! It is sad
but unfortunately true that man learns nothing from history.
This melancholy fact will present us with the greatest difficulties
as soon as we set about collecting empirical material that would
throw a little light on this dark subject, for we shall be quite
certain to find it where all the authorities have assured us that
nothing is to be found.

52 *Metaphysica vera*, Part III, "Secunda scientia," in *Opera philosophica*, ed. by
Land, II, pp. 187f.
53 *Eckermann's Conversations with Goethe*, trans. by Moon, pp. 514f. (modified).

862   Reports of remarkable isolated cases, however well authenticated, are unprofitable and lead at most to their reporter being regarded as a credulous person. Even the careful recording and verification of a large number of such cases, as in the work of Gurney, Myers, and Podmore,[54] have made next to no impression on the scientific world. The great majority of "professional" psychologists and psychiatrists seem to be completely ignorant of these researches.[55]

*

863   The results of the ESP and PK experiments have provided a statistical basis for evaluating the phenomenon of synchronicity, and at the same time have pointed out the important part played by the psychic factor. This fact prompted me to ask whether it would not be possible to find a method which would on the one hand demonstrate the existence of synchronicity and, on the other hand, disclose psychic contents which would at least give us a clue to the nature of the psychic factor involved. I asked myself, in other words, whether there were not a method which would yield measurable results and at the same time give us an insight into the psychic background of synchronicity. That there are certain essential psychic conditions for synchronistic phenomena we have already seen from the ESP experiments, although the latter are in the nature of the case restricted to the fact of coincidence and only stress its psychic background without illuminating it any further. I had known for a long time that there were intuitive or "mantic" methods which start with the psychic factor and take the existence of synchronicity as self-evident. I therefore turned my attention first of all to the intuitive technique for *grasping the total situation* which is so characteristic of China, namely the *I Ching* or *Book of Changes.*[56] Unlike the Greek-trained Western mind, the Chinese mind does not aim at grasping details for their own sake, but at a view which sees the detail as part of a whole. For obvious

[54] See p. 14, supra.

[55] Recently Pascual Jordan has put up an excellent case for the scientific investigation of spatial clairvoyance ("Positivistische Bemerkungen über die parapsychischen Erscheinungen"). I would also draw attention to his *Verdrängung und Komplementarität,* concerning the relations between microphysics and the psychology of the unconscious.

[56] Trans. by Cary F. Baynes from the Richard Wilhelm translation.

reasons, a cognitive operation of this kind is impossible to the unaided intellect. Judgment must therefore rely much more on the irrational functions of consciousness, that is on sensation (the "sens du réel") and intuition (perception by means of subliminal contents). The *I Ching*, which we can well call the experimental foundation of classical Chinese philosophy, is one of the oldest known methods for grasping a situation as a whole and thus placing the details against a cosmic background—the interplay of Yin and Yang.

864   This grasping of the whole is obviously the aim of science as well, but it is a goal that necessarily lies very far off because science, whenever possible, proceeds experimentally and in all cases statistically. Experiment, however, consists in asking a definite question which excludes as far as possible anything disturbing and irrelevant. It makes conditions, imposes them on Nature, and in this way forces her to give an answer to a question devised by man. She is prevented from answering out of the fullness of her possibilities since these possibilities are restricted as far as practicable. For this purpose there is created in the laboratory a situation which is artificially restricted to the question and which compels Nature to give an unequivocal answer. The workings of Nature in her unrestricted wholeness are completely excluded. If we want to know what these workings are, we need a method of inquiry which imposes the fewest possible conditions, or if possible no conditions at all, and then leaves Nature to answer out of her fullness.

865   In the laboratory experiment, the known and established procedure forms the stable factor in the statistical compilation and comparison of the results. In the intuitive or "mantic" experiment-with-the-whole, on the other hand, there is no need of any question which imposes conditions and restricts the wholeness of the natural process. It is given every possible chance to express itself. In the *I Ching* the coins fall just as happens to suit them.[57] From the point of view of an observer, an unknown question is followed by a rationally unintelligible answer. Thus far the conditions for a total reaction are positively ideal. The disadvantage, however, leaps to the eye: in contrast to the scientific experiment one does not know what

57 If the experiment is made with the traditional yarrow stalks, the division of the forty-nine stalks represents the chance factor.

has happened. To overcome this drawback, two Chinese sages, King Wên and the Duke of Chou, in the twelfth century before our era, basing themselves on the hypothesis of the unity of nature, sought to explain the simultaneous occurrence of a psychic state with a physical process as *an equivalence of meaning*. In other words, they supposed that the same living reality was expressing itself in the psychic state as in the physical. But, in order to verify such an hypothesis, *some* limiting condition was needed in this apparently limitless experiment, namely a definite form of physical procedure, a method or technique which forced nature to answer in even and odd numbers. These, as representatives of Yin and Yang, are found both in the unconscious and in nature in the characteristic form of opposites, as the "mother" and "father" of everything that happens, and they therefore form the *tertium comparationis* between the psychic inner world and the physical outer world. Thus the two sages devised a method by which an inner state could be represented as an outer one and vice versa. This naturally presupposes an intuitive knowledge of the meaning of each oracle figure. The *I Ching*, therefore, consists of a collection of sixty-four interpretations in which the meaning of each of the possible Yin-Yang combinations is worked out. These interpretations formulate the inner unconscious knowledge that corresponds to the state of consciousness at the moment, and this psychological situation coincides with the chance results of the method, that is, with the odd and even numbers resulting from the fall of the coins or the division of the yarrow stalks.[58]

866   The method, like all divinatory or intuitive techniques, is based on an acausal or synchronistic connective principle.[59] In practice, as any unprejudiced person will admit, many obvious cases of synchronicity occur during the experiment, which could be rationally and somewhat arbitrarily explained away as mere projections. But if one assumes that they really are what they

[58] See also infra, par. 986.

[59] I first used this term in my memorial address for Richard Wilhelm (delivered May 10, 1930, in Munich). The address later appeared as an appendix to *The Secret of the Golden Flower*, where I said: "The science of the *I Ching* is not based on the causality principle, but on a principle (hitherto unnamed because not met with among us) which I have tentatively called the synchronistic principle" (p. 141). [Cf. "Richard Wilhelm: In Memoriam," par. 81.]

appear to be, then they can only be meaningful coincidences for which, as far as we know, there is no causal explanation. The method consists either in dividing the forty-nine yarrow stalks into two heaps at random and counting off the heaps by threes and fives, or in throwing three coins six times, each line of the hexagram being determined by the value of obverse and reverse (heads 3, tails 2).[60] The experiment is based on a triadic principle (two trigrams) and contains sixty-four mutations, each corresponding to a psychic situation. These are discussed at length in the text and appended commentaries. There is also a Western method of very ancient origin [61] which is based on the same general principle as the *I Ching,* the only difference being that in the West this principle is not triadic but, significantly enough, tetradic, and the result is not a hexagram built up of Yang and Yin lines but sixteen figures composed of odd and even numbers. Twelve of them are arranged, according to certain rules, in the astrological houses. The experiment is based on 4×4 lines consisting of a random number of points which the questioner marks in the sand or on paper from right to left.[62] In true Occidental fashion the combination of all these factors goes into considerably more detail than the *I Ching.* Here too there are any amount of meaningful coincidences, but they are as a rule harder to understand and therefore less obvious than in the latter. In the Western method, which was known since the thirteenth century as the *Ars Geomantica* or the Art of Punctation [63] and enjoyed a widespread vogue, there are no real commentaries, since its use was only mantic and never philosophical like that of the *I Ching.*

867 Though the results of both procedures point in the desired direction, they do not provide any basis for a statistical evaluation. I have, therefore, looked round for another intuitive technique and have hit on astrology, which, at least in its modern form, claims to give a more or less total picture of the individual's character. There is no lack of commentaries here; indeed,

---

[60] *I Ching,* pp. 721f.
[61] Mentioned by Isidore of Seville in his *Liber etymologiarum,* VIII, ix, 13.
[62] Grains of corn or dice can also be used.
[63] The best account is to be found in Robert Fludd (1574–1637), *De arte geomantica.* Cf. Lynn Thorndike, *A History of Magic and Experimental Science,* II, p. 110.

we find a bewildering profusion of them—a sure sign that interpretation is neither simple nor certain. The meaningful coincidence we are looking for is immediately apparent in astrology, since the astronomical data are said by astrologers to correspond to individual traits of character; from the remotest times the various planets, houses, zodiacal signs, and aspects have all had meanings that serve as a basis for a character study or for an interpretation of a given situation. It is always possible to object that the result does not agree with our psychological knowledge of the situation or character in question, and it is difficult to refute the assertion that knowledge of character is a highly subjective affair, because in characterology there are no infallible or even reliable signs that can be in any way measured or calculated—an objection that also applies to graphology, although in practice it enjoys widespread recognition.

868 This criticism, together with the absence of reliable criteria for determining traits of character, makes the meaningful coincidence of horoscope structure and individual character postulated by astrology seem inapplicable for the purpose here under discussion. If, therefore, we want astrology to tell us anything about the acausal connection of events, we must discard this uncertain diagnosis of character and put in its place an absolutely certain and indubitable fact. One such fact is the marriage connection between two persons.[64]

869 Since antiquity, the main traditional astrological and alchemical correspondence to marriage has been the *coniunctio Solis* (☉) *et Lunae* (☽), the *coniunctio Lunae et Lunae,* and the conjunction of the moon with the ascendent.[65] There are others, but these do not come within the main traditional

[64] Other obvious facts would be murder and suicide. Statistics are to be found in Herbert von Kloeckler (*Astrologie als Erfahrungswissenschaft*, pp. 232ff. and 260ff.), but unfortunately they fail to give comparisons with normal average values and cannot be used for our purpose. On the other hand, Paul Flambart (*Preuves et bases de l'astrologie scientifique*, pp. 79ff.) shows a graph of statistics on the ascendents of 123 outstandingly intelligent people. Definite accumulations occur at the corners of the airy trigon (♊, ♎, ♒). This result was confirmed by a further 300 cases.

[65] This view dates back to Ptolemy: "Apponit [Ptolemaeus] autem tres gradus concordiae: Primus cum Sol in viro, et Sol vel Luna in femina, aut Luna in utrisque, fuerint in locis se respicientibus trigono, vel hexagono aspectu. Secundus cum in viro Luna, in uxore Sol eodem modo disponuntur. Tertius si cum hoc

stream. The ascendent-descendent axis was introduced into the tradition because it has long been regarded as having a particularly important influence on the personality.[66] As I shall refer later to the conjunction and opposition of Mars (♂) and Venus (♀), I may say here that these are related to marriage only because the conjunction or opposition of these two planets points to a love relationship, and this may or may not produce a marriage. So far as my experiment is concerned, we have to investigate the coincident aspects ☉ ☾ , ☾ ☾ , and ☾ *Asc.* in the horoscopes of married pairs in relation to those of unmarried pairs. It will, further, be of interest to compare the relation of the above aspects to those of the aspects which belong only in a minor degree to the main traditional stream. No belief in astrology is needed to carry out such an investigation, only the birth-dates, an astronomical almanac, and a table of logarithms for working out the horoscope.

---

alter alterum recipiat." (Ptolemy postulates three degrees of harmony. The first is when the sun in the man's [horoscope], and the sun or moon in the woman's, or the moon in both, are in their respective places in a trine or sextile aspect. The second degree is when the moon in a man's [horoscope] and the sun in a woman's are constellated in the same way. The third degree is when the one is receptive to the other.) On the same page, Cardan quotes Ptolemy (*De iudiciis astrorum*): "Omnino vero constantes et diurni convictus permanent quando in utriusque genitura conjugis luminaria contigerit configurata esse concorditer" (Generally speaking, their life together will be long and constant when in the horoscopes of both partners the luminaries [sun and moon] are harmoniously constellated). Ptolemy regards the conjunction of a masculine moon with a feminine sun as particularly favourable for marriage.—Jerome Cardan, *Commentaria in Ptolemaeum de astrorum iudiciis*, Book IV (in his *Opera omnia*, V, p. 332).

66 The practising astrologer can hardly suppress a smile here, because for him these correspondences are absolutely self-evident, a classic example being Goethe's connection with Christiane Vulpius: ☉ 5⁰ ♍ ♂ ☾ 7⁰ ♍.

I should perhaps add a few explanatory words for those readers who do not feel at home with the ancient art and technique of astrology. Its basis is the horoscope, a circular arrangement of sun, moon, and planets according to their relative positions in the signs of the zodiac at the moment of an individual's birth. There are three main positions, viz., those of sun (☉), moon (☾), and the so-called ascendent (*Asc.*); the last has the greatest importance for the interpretation of a nativity: the *Asc.* represents the degree of the zodiacal sign rising over the eastern horizon at the moment of birth. The horoscope consists of 12 so-called "houses," sectors of 30° each. Astrological tradition ascribes different qualities to them as it does to the various "aspects," i.e., angular relations of the planets and the *luminaria* (sun ☉ and moon ☾), and to the zodiacal signs.

870   As the above three mantic procedures show, the method best adapted to the nature of chance is the numerical method. Since the remotest times men have used numbers to establish meaningful coincidences, that is, coincidences that can be interpreted. There is something peculiar, one might even say mysterious, about numbers. They have never been entirely robbed of their numinous aura. If, so a text-book of mathematics tells us, a group of objects is deprived of every single one of its properties or characteristics, there still remains, at the end, its *number,* which seems to indicate that number is something irreducible. (I am not concerned here with the logic of this mathematical argument, but only with its psychology!) The sequence of natural numbers turns out to be unexpectedly more than a mere stringing together of identical units: it contains the whole of mathematics and everything yet to be discovered in this field. Number, therefore, is in one sense an unpredictable entity. Although I would not care to undertake to say anything illuminating about the inner relation between two such apparently incommensurable things as number and synchronicity, I cannot refrain from pointing out that not only were they always brought into connection with one another, but that both possess numinosity and mystery as their common characteristics. Number has invariably been used to characterize some numinous object, and all numbers from 1 to 9 are "sacred," just as 10, 12, 13, 14, 28, 32, and 40 have a special significance. The most elementary quality about an object is whether it is one or many. Number helps more than anything else to bring order into the chaos of appearances. It is the predestined instrument for creating order, or for apprehending an already existing, but still unknown, regular arrangement or "orderedness." It may well be the most primitive element of order in the human mind, seeing that the numbers 1 to 4 occur with the greatest frequency and have the widest incidence. In other words, primitive patterns of order are mostly triads or tetrads. That numbers have an archetypal foundation is not, by the way, a conjecture of mine but of certain mathematicians, as we shall see in due course. Hence it is not such an audacious conclusion after all if we define number psychologically as an *archetype of order* which has become conscious.[67] Remarkably enough, the psychic

[67] Cf. "On the Psychology of Eastern Meditation," par. 942.

images of wholeness which are spontaneously produced by the unconscious, the symbols of the self in mandala form, also have a mathematical structure. They are as a rule quaternities (or their multiples).[68] These structures not only express order, they also create it. That is why they generally appear in times of psychic disorientation in order to compensate a chaotic state or as formulations of numinous experiences. It must be emphasized yet again that they are not inventions of the conscious mind but are spontaneous products of the unconscious, as has been sufficiently shown by experience. Naturally the conscious mind can imitate these patterns of order, but such imitations do not prove that the originals are conscious inventions. From this it follows irrefutably that the unconscious uses number as an ordering factor.

871   It is generally believed that numbers were *invented* or thought out by man, and are therefore nothing but concepts of quantities, containing nothing that was not previously put into them by the human intellect. But it is equally possible that numbers were *found* or discovered. In that case they are not only concepts but something more—autonomous entities which somehow contain more than just quantities. Unlike concepts, they are based not on any psychic conditions but on the quality of being themselves, on a "so-ness" that cannot be expressed by an intellectual concept. Under these conditions they might easily be endowed with qualities that have still to be discovered. I must confess that I incline to the view that numbers were as much found as invented, and that in consequence they possess a relative autonomy analogous to that of the archetypes. They would then have, in common with the latter, the quality of being pre-existent to consciousness, and hence, on occasion, of conditioning it rather than being conditioned by it. The archetypes too, as *a priori* forms of representation, are as much found as invented: they are *discovered* inasmuch as one did not know of their unconscious autonomous existence, and *invented* inasmuch as their presence was inferred from analogous representational structures. Accordingly it would seem that natural numbers have an archetypal character. If that is so, then not only would certain numbers and combinations of numbers have a relation

68 Cf. "A Study in the Process of Individuation" and "Concerning Mandala Symbolism."

41

to and an effect on certain archetypes, but the reverse would also be true. The first case is equivalent to number magic, but the second is equivalent to inquiring whether numbers, in conjunction with the combination of archetypes found in astrology, would show a tendency to behave in a special way.

2. AN ASTROLOGICAL EXPERIMENT

872   As I have already said, we need two different facts, one of which represents the astrological constellation, and the other the married state.

873   The material to be examined, namely a quantity of marriage horoscopes, was obtained from friendly donors in Zurich, London, Rome, and Vienna. Originally the material had been put together for purely astrological purposes, some of it many years ago, so that those who gathered the material knew of no connection between its collection and the aim of the present study, a fact which I stress because it might be objected that the material was specially selected with that aim in view. This was not so; the sample was a random one. The horoscopes, or rather the birth data, were piled up in chronological order just as the post brought them in. When the horoscopes of 180 married pairs had come in, there was a pause in the collection, during which the 360 horoscopes were worked out. This first batch was used to conduct a pilot investigation, as I wanted to test out the methods to be employed.

874   Since the material had been collected originally in order to test the empirical foundations of this intuitive method, a few more general remarks may not be out of place concerning the considerations which prompted the collection of the material.

875   Marriage is a well-characterized fact, though its psychological

43

aspect shows every conceivable sort of variation. According to the astrological view, it is precisely this aspect of marriage that expresses itself most markedly in the horoscopes. The possibility that the individuals characterized by the horoscopes married one another, so to say, by accident will necessarily recede into the background; all external factors seem capable of astrological evaluation, but only inasmuch as they are represented psychologically. Owing to the very large number of characterological variations, we would hardly expect marriage to be characterized by only *one* astrological configuration; rather, if astrological assumptions are at all correct, there will be several configurations that point to a predisposition in the choice of a marriage partner. In this connection I must call the reader's attention to the well-known correspondence between the sun-spot periods and the mortality curve. The connecting link appears to be the disturbances of the earth's magnetic field, which in their turn are due to fluctuations in the proton radiation from the sun. These fluctuations also have an influence on "radio weather" by disturbing the ionosphere that reflects the radio waves.[1] Investigation of these disturbances seems to indicate that the conjunctions, oppositions, and quartile aspects of the planets play a considerable part in increasing the proton radiation and thus causing electromagnetic storms. On the other hand, the astrologically favourable trine and sextile aspects have been reported to produce uniform radio weather.

876   These observations give us an unexpected glimpse into a possible causal basis for astrology. At all events, this is certainly true of Kepler's weather astrology. But it is also possible that, over and above the already established physiological effects of proton radiation, psychic effects can occur which would rob astrological statements of their chance nature and bring them within range of a causal explanation. Although nobody knows what the validity of a nativity horoscope rests on, it is just conceivable that there is a causal connection between the planetary aspects and the psycho-physiological disposition. One would therefore do well not to regard the results of astrological observation as synchronistic phenomena, but to take them as

1 For a comprehensive account of this, see Max Knoll, "Transformations of Science in Our Age," in *Man and Time*.

possibly causal in origin. For, wherever a cause is even remotely thinkable, synchronicity becomes an exceedingly doubtful proposition.

877   For the present, at any rate, we have insufficient grounds for believing that the astrological results are more than mere chance, or that statistics involving large numbers yield a statistically significant result.[2] As large-scale studies are lacking, I decided to investigate the empirical basis of astrology, using a large number of horoscopes of married pairs just to see what kind of figures would turn up.

Pilot Investigation

878   With the first batch assembled, I turned first to the conjunctions (☌) and oppositions (☍) of sun and moon,[3] two aspects

Male

		☉	☽	♂	♀	Asc.	Desc.
	☉	☌ ☍	☌ ☍	☌ ☍	☍ ☌	☌	☌
	☽	☌ ☍	☌ ☍	☍ ☌	☌ ☍	☌	☌
Female	♂	☍ ☌	☌ ☍	☌ ☍	☌ ☍	☌	☌
	♀	☌ ☍	☍ ☌	☌ ☍	☍ ☌	☌	☌
	Asc.	☌	☌	☌	☌	☌	☌
	Desc.	☌	☌	☌	☌		

☌ = conjunction   ☍ = opposition

FIG. 1

2 Cf. the statistical results in K. E. Krafft and others, *Le Premier Traité d'astro-biologie*, pp. 23ff. and passim.

3 Although the quartile, trine and sextile aspects and the relations to the Medium and Imum Coeli ought really to be considered, I have omitted them here so as not to make the exposition unduly complicated. The main point is not *what* marriage aspects are, but whether they can be detected in the horoscope.

regarded in astrology as being about equally strong (though in opposite senses), i.e., as signifying intensive relations between the heavenly bodies. Together with the δ, φ, *Asc.*, and *Desc.* conjunctions and oppositions, they yield fifty different aspects.[4]

879   The reasons why I chose these combinations will be clear to the reader from my remarks on the astrological traditions in the previous chapter. I have only to add here that, of the conjunctions and oppositions, those of Mars and Venus are far less important than the rest, as will readily be appreciated from the following consideration: the relation of Mars to Venus can reveal a love relation, but a marriage is not always a love relation and a love relation is not always a marriage. My aim in including the conjunction and opposition of Mars and Venus was therefore to compare them with the other conjunctions and oppositions.

880   These fifty aspects were first studied for 180 married couples. It is clear that these 180 men and 180 women can also be paired off into unmarried couples. In fact, since any one of the 180 men could be paired off with any one of the 179 women to whom he was not married, it is clear that we can investigate $180 \times 179 = 32,220$ unmarried pairs within the group of 180 marriages. This was done (cf. Table I), and the aspect analysis for these unmarried pairs was compared with that for the married pairs. For all calculations, an orbit of 8° either way was assumed, clockwise and anticlockwise, not only inside the sign but extending beyond it. Later, two more batches of 220 and 83 marriages were added to the original batch, so that, in all, 483 marriages, or 966 horoscopes, were examined. Evaluation of the batches showed that the most frequent aspect in the first was a sun-moon conjunction (10%), in the second a moon-moon conjunction (10.9%), and in the third a moon-*Asc.* conjunction (9.6%).

881   To begin with, what interested me most was, of course, the question of probability: were the maximum results that we obtained "significant" figures or not?—that is, were they improbable or not? Calculations undertaken by a mathematician showed unmistakably that the average frequency of 10% in all three batches is far from representing a significant figure. Its

4 Fig. 1 (p. 461) sets out clearly the 50 different aspects as they actually occurred in the 180 married pairs.

probability is much too great; in other words, there is no ground for assuming that our maximum frequencies are more than mere dispersions due to chance.

Analysis of First Batch

882   First we counted all the conjunctions and oppositions between ☉ ☽ ♂ ♀ *Asc.* and *Desc.* for the 180 married and the 32,220 unmarried pairs. The results are shown in Table I, where it will be observed that the aspects are arranged by frequency of their occurrence in the married and unmarried pairs.

883   Clearly, the frequencies of occurrence shown in columns 2 and 4 of Table I for observed occurrences of the aspects in married and unmarried pairs respectively are not immediately comparable, since the first are occurrences in 180 pairs and the second in 32,220 pairs.[5] In column 5, therefore, we show the figures in column 4 multiplied by the factor $\frac{180}{32,220}$. Table II shows the ratios between the figures in columns 2 and 5 of Table I arranged according to frequency; e.g., the ratio for moon-sun conjunction is $18 : 8.4 = 2.14$.

884   To a statistician, these figures cannot be used to confirm anything, and so are valueless, because they are chance dispersions. But on psychological grounds I have discarded the idea that we are dealing with *mere* chance numbers. In a total picture of natural events, it is just as important to consider the exceptions to the rule as the averages. This is the fallacy of the statistical picture: it is one-sided, inasmuch as it represents only the average aspect of reality and excludes the total picture. The statistical view of the world is a mere abstraction and therefore incomplete and even fallacious, particularly so when it deals with man's psychology. Inasmuch as chance maxima and minima occur, they are *facts* whose nature I set out to explore.

5 [In this way a rough control group is obtained. It will, however, be appreciated that it is derived from a much larger number of pairs than the married pairs: 32,220 as compared with 180. This leads to the possibility of showing the chance nature of the 180 pairs. On the hypothesis that all the figures are due to chance, we would expect a far greater accuracy in the greater number and consequently a much smaller range in the figures. This is so, for the range in the 180 married pairs is $18 - 2 = 16$, whereas in the 180 unmarried pairs we get $9.6 - 7.4 = 2.2$. —Editors.]

TABLE I

Fem.	Aspect	Masc.	Observed Occurrences for 180 Married Pairs		Observed Occurrences for 32,220 Unmarried Pairs	Calculated Frequency for 180 Unmarried Pairs	
			Actual Occurrences	Percentage Occurrences		Actual Frequency	Frequency Percentage
Moon	♂	Sun	18	10.0%	1506	8.4	4.7
Asc.	♂	Venus	15	8.3%	1411	7.9	4.4
Moon	♂	Asc.	14	7.7%	1485	8.3	4.6
Moon	☍	Sun	13	7.2%	1438	8.0	4.4
Moon	♂	Moon	13	7.2%	1479	8.3	4.6
Venus	☍	Moon	13	7.2%	1526	8.5	4.7
Mars	♂	Moon	13	7.2%	1548	8.6	4.8
Mars	♂	Mars	13	7.2%	1711	9.6	5.3
Mars	♂	Asc.	12	6.6%	1467	8.2	4.6
Sun	♂	Mars	12	6.6%	1485	8.3	4.6
Venus	♂	Asc.	11	6.1%	1409	7.9	4.4
Sun	♂	Asc.	11	6.1%	1413	7.9	4.4
Mars	♂	Desc.	11	6.1%	1471	8.2	4.6
Desc.	♂	Venus	11	6.1%	1470	8.2	4.6
Venus	♂	Desc.	11	6.1%	1526	8.5	4.7
Moon	☍	Mars	10	5.5%	1540	8.6	4.8
Venus	☍	Venus	9	5.0%	1415	7.9	4.4
Venus	♂	Mars	9	5.0%	1498	8.4	4.7
Venus	♂	Sun	9	5.0%	1526	8.5	4.7
Moon	♂	Mars	9	5.0%	1539	8.6	4.8
Sun	♂	Desc.	9	5.0%	1556	8.7	4.8
Asc.	♂	Asc.	9	5.0%	1595	8.9	4.9
Desc.	♂	Sun	8	4.3%	1398	7.8	4.3
Venus	☍	Sun	8	4.3%	1485	8.3	4.6
Sun	♂	Moon	8	4.3%	1508	8.4	4.7

TABLE I (*continued*)

Aspect			Observed Occurrences for 180 Married Pairs		Observed Occurrences for 32,220 Unmarried Pairs	Calculated Frequency for 180 Unmarried Pairs	
Fem.		Masc.	Actual Occurrences	Percentage Occurrences		Actual Frequency	Frequency Percentage
Sun	☍	Venus	8	4.3%	1502	8.4	4.7
Sun	☍	Mars	8	4.3%	1516	8.5	4.7
Mars	☍	Sun	8	4.3%	1516	8.5	4.7
Mars	☌	Venus	8	4.3%	1520	8.5	4.7
Venus	☍	Mars	8	4.3%	1531	8.6	4.8
Asc.	☌	Moon	8	4.3%	1541	8.6	4.8
Moon	☍	Moon	8	4.3%	1548	8.6	4.8
Desc.	☌	Moon	8	4.3%	1543	8.6	4.8
Asc.	☌	Mars	8	4.3%	1625	9.1	5.0
Moon	☌	Venus	7	3.8%	1481	8.3	4.6
Mars	☍	Venus	7	3.8%	1521	8.5	4.7
Moon	☌	Desc.	7	3.8%	1539	8.6	4.8
Mars	☍	Moon	7	3.8%	1540	8.6	4.8
Asc.	☌	Desc.	6	3.3%	1328	7.4	4.1
Desc.	☌	Mars	6	3.3%	1433	8.0	4.4
Venus	☌	Moon	6	3.3%	1436	8.0	4.4
Asc.	☌	Sun	6	3.3%	1587	8.9	4.9
Mars	☌	Sun	6	3.3%	1575	8.8	4.9
Moon	☍	Venus	6	3.3%	1576	8.8	4.9
Venus	☌	Venus	5	2.7%	1497	8.4	4.7
Sun	☍	Moon	5	2.7%	1530	8.6	4.8
Sun	☌	Venus	4	2.2%	1490	8.3	4.6
Mars	☍	Mars	3	1.6%	1440	8.0	4.4
Sun	☌	Sun	2	1.1%	1480	8.3	4.6
Sun	☍	Sun	2	1.1%	1482	8.3	4.6

TABLE II

Fem.	Aspect	Masc.	Proportion of Aspect Frequencies for Married Pairs	Fem.	Aspect	Masc.	Proportion of Aspect Frequencies for Married Pairs
Moon	☌	Sun	2.14	Sun	☍	Venus	0.95
Asc.	☌	Venus	1.89	Sun	☍	Mars	0.94
Moon	☌	Asc.	1.68	Mars	☍	Sun	0.94
Moon	☍	Sun	1.61	Mars	☌	Venus	0.94
Moon	☌	Moon	1.57	Venus	☍	Mars	0.94
Venus	☍	Moon	1.53	Asc.	☌	Moon	0.93
Mars	☌	Moon	1.50	Moon	☍	Moon	0.93
Mars	☌	Asc.	1.46	Desc.	☌	Moon	0.92
Sun	☌	Mars	1.44	Asc.	☌	Mars	0.88
Venus	☌	Asc.	1.39	Moon	☌	Venus	0.85
Sun	☌	Asc.	1.39	Mars	☍	Venus	0.82
Mars	☌	Mars	1.36	Moon	☌	Desc.	0.81
Mars	☌	Desc.	1.34	Asc.	☌	Desc.	0.81
Desc.	☌	Venus	1.34	Mars	☍	Moon	0.81
Venus	☌	Desc.	1.29	Desc.	☌	Mars	0.75
Moon	☍	Mars	1.16	Venus	☌	Moon	0.75
Venus	☍	Venus	1.14	Asc.	☌	Sun	0.68
Venus	☌	Mars	1.07	Mars	☌	Sun	0.68
Venus	☌	Sun	1.06	Moon	☍	Venus	0.68
Moon	☌	Mars	1.05	Venus	☌	Venus	0.60
Sun	☌	Desc.	1.04	Sun	☍	Moon	0.59
Desc.	☌	Sun	1.02	Sun	☌	Venus	0.48
Asc.	☌	Asc.	1.01	Mars	☍	Mars	0.37
Venus	☍	Sun	0.96	Sun	☌	Sun	0.24
Sun	☌	Moon	0.95	Sun	☍	Sun	0.24

885   What strikes us in Table II is the unequal distribution of the frequency values. The top seven and bottom six aspects both show a fairly strong dispersion, while the middle values tend to cluster round the ratio 1 : 1. I shall come back to this peculiar distribution with the help of a special graph (Fig. 2).

886   An interesting point is the confirmation of the traditional astrological and alchemical correspondence between marriage and the moon-sun aspects:

$$\text{(fem.) moon } \mathrm{\sigma} \text{ (masc.) sun } 2.14 : 1$$
$$\text{(fem.) moon } \mathrm{\mathscr{8}} \text{ (masc.) sun } 1.61 : 1$$

whereas there is no evidence of any emphasis on the Venus-Mars aspects.

887   Of the fifty possible aspects, the result shows that for the married pairs there are fifteen such configurations whose frequency is well above the proportion 1 : 1. The highest value is found in the aforementioned moon-sun conjunction, and the two next-highest figures—1.89 : 1 and 1.68 : 1—correspond to the conjunctions between (fem.) *Asc.* and (masc.) Venus, or (fem.) moon and (masc.) *Asc.*, thus apparently confirming the traditional significance of the ascendent.

888   Of these fifteen aspects, a moon aspect occurs four times for women, whereas only six moon aspects are distributed among the thirty-five other possible values. The mean proportional value of all moon aspects amounts to 1.24 : 1. The average value of the four just cited in the table amounts to 1.74 : 1, as compared with 1.24 : 1 for all moon aspects. The moon seems to be less emphasized for men than for women.

889   For men the corresponding role is played not by the sun but by the *Asc.-Desc.* axis. In the first fifteen aspects of Table II, these aspects occur six times for men and only twice for women. In the former case they have an average value of 1.42 : 1, as compared with 1.22 : 1 for all masculine aspects between *Asc.* or *Desc.* on the one hand and one of the four heavenly bodies on the other.

890   Figures 2 and 3 give a graphic representation of the frequencies shown respectively in columns 2 and 5 of Table I from the point of view of the dispersion of aspects.

891   This arrangement enables us not only to visualize the dispersion in the frequency of occurrence of the different aspects but also to make a rapid estimate of the mean number of occurrences per aspect, using the median as an estimator. Whereas, in order to get the arithmetic mean, we have to total the aspect frequencies and divide by the number of aspects, the median

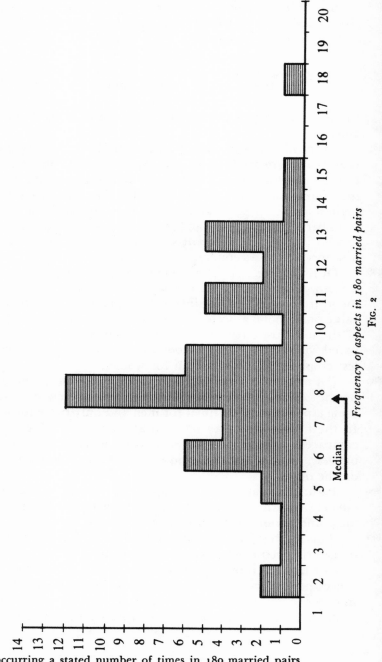

Frequency of aspects in 180 married pairs

Fig. 2

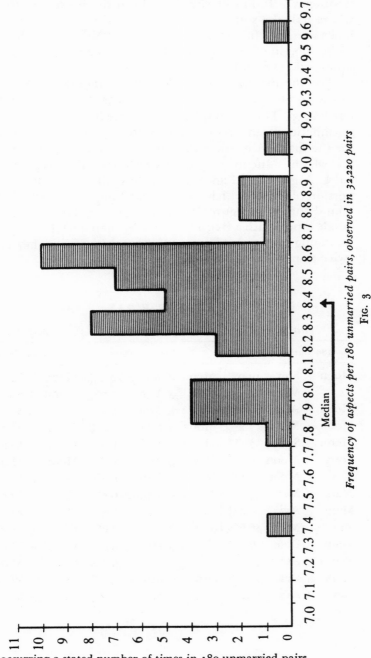

Aspects occurring a stated number of times in 180 unmarried pairs

Frequency of aspects per 180 unmarried pairs, observed in 32,220 pairs

FIG. 3

frequency is found by counting down the histogram to a point where half the squares are counted and half are still to count. Since there are fifty squares in the histogram, the median is seen to be 8.0, since 25 squares do not exceed this value and 25 squares do exceed it (cf. Fig. 2).

892   For the married pairs the median amounts to 8 cases, but in the combinations of unmarried pairs it is more, namely 8.4 (cf. Fig. 3). For the unmarried the median coincides with the arithmetic mean—both amount to 8.4—whereas the median for the married is lower than the corresponding mean value of 8.4, which is due to the presence of lower values for the married pairs. A glance at Figure 2 will show that there is a wide dispersion of values which contrasts strikingly with those clustered round the mean figure of 8.4 in Figure 3. Here there is not a single aspect with a frequency greater than 9.6 (cf. Fig. 3), whereas among the married one aspect reaches a frequency of nearly twice as much, namely 18 (cf. Fig. 2).

TABLE III

First Batch		Second Batch		Both Batches	
180 Married Pairs		220 Married Pairs		400 Married Pairs	
Moon ☌ Sun	10.0%	Moon ☌ Moon	10.9%	Moon ☌ Moon	9.2%
Asc. ☌ Venus	9.4%	Mars ☍ Venus	7.7%	Moon ☍ Sun	7.0%
Moon ☌ Asc.	7.7%	Venus ☌ Moon	7.2%	Moon ☌ Sun	7.0%
Moon ☌ Moon	7.2%	Moon ☍ Sun	6.8%	Mars ☌ Mars	6.2%
Moon ☍ Sun	7.2%	Moon ☍ Mars	6.8%	Desc. ☌ Venus	6.2%
Mars ☌ Moon	7.2%	Desc. ☌ Mars	6.8%	Moon ☍ Mars	6.2%
Venus ☍ Moon	7.2%	Desc. ☌ Venus	6.3%	Mars ☌ Moon	6.0%
Mars ☌ Mars	7.2%	Moon ☍ Venus	6.3%	Mars ☍ Venus	5.7%
Mars ☌ Asc.	6.6%	Venus ☌ Venus	6.3%	Moon ☌ Asc.	5.7%
Sun ☌ Mars	6.6%	Sun ☍ Mars	5.9%	Venus ☌ Desc.	5.7%
Venus ☌ Desc.	6.1%	Venus ☌ Desc.	5.4%	Venus ☌ Moon	5.5%
Venus ☌ Asc.	6.1%	Venus ☌ Mars	5.4%	Desc. ☌ Mars	5.2%
Mars ☌ Desc.	6.1%	Sun ☌ Moon	5.4%	Asc. ☌ Venus	5.2%
Sun ☌ Asc.	6.1%	Sun ☌ Sun	5.4%	Sun ☍ Mars	5.2%

Comparison of All Batches

893   On the supposition that the dispersion apparent in Figure 2 was due to chance, I investigated a larger number of marriage horoscopes by combining the first batch of 180 and the second batch of 220 married pairs, thus making 400 in all (or 800 individual horoscopes). The results are shown in Table III, though I have confined myself here to the maximal figures that clearly exceed the median. Figures are given in percentages.

894   The 180 couples in the first column represent the results of the first collection, while the 220 in the second column were collected more than a year later. The second column not only differs from the first in its aspects, but shows a marked sinking of the frequency values. The only exception is the top figure, representing the classical ☾ ☌ ☾. It takes the place of the equally classical ☾ ☌ ☉ in the first column. Of the fourteen aspects in the first column only four come up again in the second, but of these no less than three are moon aspects, and this is in accord with astrological expectations. The absence of correspondence between the aspects of the first and second columns indicates a great inequality of material, i.e., there is a wide dispersion. One can see this in the aggregate figures for the 400 married pairs: as a result of the evening out of the dispersion they all show a marked decrease. This is brought out still more clearly in Table IV, where the third batch is added.

TABLE IV

Frequency in %	☾ ☌ ☉	☾ ☌ ☾	☾ ☍ ☉	Average
180 Married Pairs	10.0	7.2	7.2	8.1
220 Married Pairs	5.4	10.9	6.8	7.7
180 + 220 = 400 Married Pairs	7.0	9.2	7.0	7.7
83 Additional Married Pairs	7.2	4.8	4.8	5.6
83 + 400 = 483 Married Pairs	7.2	8.4	6.6	7.4

895   This table shows the frequency figures for the three constellations that occur most often: two lunar conjunctions and one lunar opposition. The highest average frequency, that for the

original 180 marriages, is 8.1%; for the 220 collected and worked out later the average maximum drops to 7.7%; and for the 83 marriages that were added still later the average amounts to only 5.6%. In the original batches of 180 and 220 the maxima still lie with the same aspects, ☽ ☌ ☉ , ☽ ☌ ☽ , but in the last batch of 83 it turned out that the maxima lay with different aspects, namely Asc. ☌ ☽ , ☉ ☌ ♀ , ☉ ☌ ♂ , and Asc. ☌ Asc. The average maximum for these four aspects is 8.7%. This high figure exceeds our highest average of 8.1% for the first batch of 180, which only proves how fortuitous our "favourable" initial results were. Nevertheless it is worth pointing out that, amusingly enough, in the last batch the maximum of 9.6% lies, as we said earlier,[6] with the Asc. ☌ ☽ aspect, that is, with another lunar aspect which is supposed to be particularly characteristic of marriage. A lusus naturae, no doubt, but a very queer one, since according to tradition the ascendent or "horoscopus," together with sun and moon, forms the trinity that determines fate and character. Had one wanted to falsify the statistical findings so as to bring them into line with tradition one could not have done it more successfully.

896   Table V gives the maximal frequencies for unmarried pairs.

TABLE V

Maximal Frequency in % for

1. 300 pairs combined at random 7.3

2. 325 pairs chosen by lot 6.5

3. 400 pairs chosen by lot 6.2

4. 32,220 pairs 5.3

The first result was obtained by my co-worker, Dr. Liliane Frey-Rohn, putting the men's horoscopes on one side and the women's on the other, and then combining each of the pairs that happened to lie on top. Care was naturally taken that a real married pair was not accidentally combined. The resultant frequency of 7.3 is pretty high in comparison with the much

---

6 [Par. 880. 9.6% = 8 such aspects in 83 married pairs. See par. 902 and App., (b).— Editors.]

more probable maximal figure for the 32,220 unmarried pairs, which is only 5.3. This first result seemed to me somewhat suspicious.[7] I therefore suggested that we should not combine the pairs ourselves, but should proceed in the following way: 325 men's horoscopes were numbered, the numbers were written on separate slips, thrown into a pot, and mixed up. Then a person who knew nothing of astrology and psychology and even less of these investigations was invited to draw the slips one by one out of the pot, without looking at them. The numbers were each combined with the topmost on the pile of women's horoscopes, care being again taken that married pairs did not accidentally come together. In this way 325 artificial pairs were obtained. The resultant 6.5 is rather nearer to probability. Still more probable is the result obtained for the 400 unmarried pairs. Even so, this figure (6.2) is still too high.

897   The somewhat curious behaviour of our figures led to a further experiment whose results I mention here with all the necessary reserve, though it seems to me to throw some light on the statistical variations. It was made with three people whose psychological status was accurately known. The experiment consisted in taking 400 marriage horoscopes at random and providing 200 of them with numbers. Twenty of these were then drawn by lot by the subject. These twenty married pairs were

---

[7] How subtle these things can be is shown by the following incident: Recently it fell to my colleague to make the table arrangement for a number of people who were invited to dinner. She did this with care and discretion. But at the last moment an esteemed guest, a man, unexpectedly turned up who had at all costs to be suitably placed. The table arrangement was all upset, and a new one had to be hastily devised. There was no time for elaborate reflection. As we sat down to table, the following astrological picture manifested itself in the immediate vicinity of the guest:

LADY	LADY	GUEST	LADY
☽ in ♌	☉ in ♓	☉ in ♉	☉ in ♓
LADY	LADY	GENTLEMAN	LADY
☉ in ♌	☽ in ♓	☽ in ♉	☽ in ♓

Four ☉ ☽ marriages had arisen. My colleague, of course, had a thorough knowledge of astrological marriage aspects, and she was also acquainted with the horoscopes of the people in question. But the speed with which the new table arrangement had to be made left her no opportunity for reflection, so that the unconscious had a free hand in secretly arranging the "marriages."

examined statistically for our fifty marriage characteristics. The first subject was a woman patient who, at the time of the experiment, found herself in a state of intense emotional excitement. It proved that of twenty Mars aspects no less than ten were emphasized, with a frequency of 15.0; of the moon aspects nine, with a frequency of 10.0; and of the sun aspects nine, with a frequency of 14.0. The classical significance of Mars lies in his emotionality, in this case supported by the masculine sun. As compared with our general results there is a predominance of the Mars aspects, which fully agrees with the psychic state of the subject.

898   The second subject was a woman patient whose main problem was to realize and assert her personality in the face of her self-suppressive tendencies. In this case the axial aspects (*Asc. Desc.*), which are supposed to be characteristic of the personality, came up twelve times with a frequency of 20.0, and the moon aspects with a frequency of 18.0. This result, astrologically considered, was in full agreement with the subject's actual problems.

899   The third subject was a woman with strong inner oppositions whose union and reconciliation constituted her main problem. The moon aspects came up fourteen times with a frequency of 20.0, the sun aspects twelve times with a frequency of 15.0, and the axial aspects nine times with a frequency of 14.0. The classical *coniunctio Solis et Lunae* as the symbol of the union of opposites is clearly emphasized.

900   In all these cases the selection by lot of marriage horoscopes proves to have been influenced, and this fits in with our experience of the *I Ching* and other mantic procedures. Although all these figures lie well within the limits of probability and cannot therefore be regarded as anything more than chance, their variation, which each time corresponds surprisingly well with the psychic state of the subject, still gives one food for thought. The psychic state was characterized as a situation in which insight and decision come up against the insurmountable barrier of an unconscious opposed to the will. This relative defeat of the powers of the conscious mind constellates the moderating archetype, which appears in the first case as Mars, the emotional *maleficus*, in the second case as the equilibrating axial system that strengthens the personality, and in the third

case as the *hieros gamos* or *coniunctio* of supreme opposites.[8] The psychic and physical event (namely, the subject's problems and choice of horoscope) correspond, it would seem, to the nature of the archetype in the background and could therefore represent a synchronistic phenomenon.

901 Inasmuch as I am not very well up in the higher mathematics, and had therefore to rely on the help of a professional, I asked Professor Markus Fierz, of Basel, to calculate the probability of my maximal figures. This he very kindly did, and using the Poisson distribution he arrived at a probability of 1 : 10,000 for the first two maxima, and of 1 : 1300 for the third.[8a] Later, on checking the calculation, he found an error whose correction raised the probability of the first two maxima to 1 : 1500.[9] A further check proved the probabilities of the three maxima to be, respectively, 1 : 1000, 1 : 10,000, 1 : 50.[10] From this it is clear that although our best results— ☾ ♂ ☉ and ☾ ♂ ☾ —are fairly improbable in practice, they are theoretically so probable that there is little justification for regarding the immediate results of our statistics as anything more than chance. If for instance there is a 1 : 1000 probability of my getting the telephone connection I want, I shall probably prefer, instead of waiting on the off-chance for a telephone conversation, to write a letter. Our investigation shows that not only do the frequency values approximate to the average with the greatest number of married pairs, but that any chance pairings produce similar statistical proportions. From the scientific point of view the result of our investigation is in some respects not encouraging for astrology, as everything seems to indicate that in the case of large numbers the differences between the frequency values for the marriage aspects of married and unmarried pairs disappear altogether. Thus, from the scientific

---

[8] Cf. the nuptials of sun and moon in alchemy: *Psychology and Alchemy,* index, *s.v.* "Sol and Luna."   [8a] [See infra, pars. 989–91.—EDITORS.]

[9] Professor Fierz wishes to correct this sentence as follows: "Later on he called my attention to the fact that the sequence of the 3 aspects does not matter. As there are 6 possible sequences, we have to multiply our probability by 6, which gives 1 : 1500." To this I reply that I never suggested anything of the kind! The sequence, i.e., the way in which the 3 conjunctions follow each other, has no importance at all.

[10] [See App., (b). This passage has been rewritten to include the three sets of probabilities supplied by Professor Fierz.—EDITORS.]

point of view, there is little hope of proving that astrological correspondence is something that conforms to law. At the same time, it is not so easy to counter the astrologer's objection that my statistical method is too arbitrary and too clumsy to evaluate correctly the numerous psychological and astrological aspects of marriage.

902   So the essential thing that remains over from our astrological statistics is the fact that the first batch of 180 marriage horoscopes shows a distinct maximum of 18 for ☽ ☌ ☉ and the second batch of 220 a maximum of 24 for ☽ ☌ ♄. These two aspects have long been mentioned in the old literature as marriage characteristics, and they therefore represent the oldest tradition. The third batch of 83 yields a maximum of 8 for ☽ ☌ *Asc.* These maxima, as we have said, have probabilities of about 1 : 1000, 1 : 10,000, and 1 : 50 respectively. I should like to illustrate what has happened here by means of an example:

You take three matchboxes, put 1,000 black ants in the first, 10,000 in the second and 50 in the third, together with one white ant in each, shut the boxes, and bore a hole in each of them, small enough to allow only one ant to crawl through at a time. The first ant to come out of each of the three boxes is always the white one.

903   The chances of this actually happening are extremely improbable. Even in the first two cases, the probability works out at 1 : 1000 $\times$ 10,000, which means that such a coincidence is to be expected only in one case out of 10,000,000. It is improbable that it would ever happen in anyone's experience. Yet in my statistical investigation it happened that precisely the three conjunctions stressed by astrological tradition came together in the most improbable way.

904   For the sake of accuracy, however, it should be pointed out that it is not the *same* white ant that is the first to appear each time. That is to say, although there is always a lunar conjunction and always a "classical" one of decisive significance, they are nevertheless different conjunctions, because each time the moon is associated with a different partner. These are of course the three main components of the horoscope, namely the ascendent, or rising degree of a zodiacal sign, which characterizes the moment, the moon, which characterizes the day, and the sun, which characterizes the month of birth. Hence, if we consider only the first two batches, we must assume two white ants

for each box. This correction raises the probability of the coinciding lunar conjunctions to 1 : 2,500,000. If we take the third batch as well, the coincidence of the three classical moon aspects has a probability of 1 : 62,500,000. The first proportion is significant even when taken by itself, for it shows that the coincidence is a very improbable one. But the coincidence with the third lunar conjunction is so remarkable that it looks like a deliberate arrangement in favour of astrology. If, therefore, the result of our experiment should be found to have a significant—i.e., more than merely chance—probability, the case for astrology would be proved in the most satisfactory way. If, on the contrary, the figures actually fall within the limits of chance expectation, they do not support the astrological claim, they merely *imitate* accidentally the ideal answer to astrological expectation. It is nothing but a chance result from the statistical point of view, yet it is *meaningful* on account of the fact that it looks as if it validated this expectation. It is just what I call a synchronistic phenomenon. The statistically significant statement only concerns regularly occurring events, and if considered as axiomatic, it simply abolishes all exceptions to the rule. It produces a merely average picture of natural events, but not a *true* picture of the world as it is. Yet the exceptions—and my results are exceptions and most improbable ones at that—are just as important as the rules. Statistics would not even make sense without the exceptions. There is no rule that is true under all circumstances, for this is the real and not a statistical world. Because the statistical method shows only the average aspects, it creates an artificial and predominantly conceptual picture of reality. That is why we need a complementary principle for a complete description and explanation of nature.

905   If we now consider the results of Rhine's experiments, and particularly the fact that they depend in large measure on the subject's active interest,[11] we can regard what happened in our case as a synchronistic phenomenon. The statistical material shows that a practically as well as theoretically improbable chance combination occurred which coincides in the most remarkable way with traditional astrological expectations. That

11 Cf. G. Schmiedler, "Personality Correlates of ESP as Shown by Rorschach Studies." The author points out that those who accept the possibility of ESP get results above expectation, whereas those who reject it get negative results.

such a coincidence should occur at all is so improbable and so incredible that nobody could have dared to predict anything like it. It really does look as if the statistical material had been manipulated and arranged so as to give the appearance of a positive result. The necessary emotional and archetypal conditions for a synchronistic phenomenon were already given, since it is obvious that both my co-worker and myself had a lively interest in the outcome of the experiment, and apart from that the question of synchronicity had been engaging my attention for many years. What seems in fact to have happened—and seems often to have happened, bearing in mind the long astrological tradition—is that we got a result which has presumably turned up many times before in history. Had the astrologers (with but few exceptions) concerned themselves more with statistics and questioned the justice of their interpretations in a scientific spirit, they would have discovered long ago that their statements rested on a precarious foundation. But I imagine that in their case too, as with me, a secret, mutual connivance existed between the material and the psychic state of the astrologer. This correspondence is simply *there* like any other agreeable or annoying accident, and it seems doubtful to me whether it can be proved scientifically to be anything more than that.[12] One may be fooled by coincidence, but one has to have a very thick skin not to be impressed by the fact that, out of fifty possibilities, three times precisely those turned up as maxima which are regarded by tradition as typical.

906   As though to make this startling result even more impressive, we found that use had been made of unconscious deception. On first working out the statistics I was put off the trail by a number of errors which I fortunately discovered in time. After overcoming this difficulty I then forgot to mention, in the Swiss edition of this book, that the ant comparison, if applied to our experiment, only fits if respectively two or three white ants are assumed each time. This considerably reduces the improbability of our results. Then, at the eleventh hour, Professor Fierz, on

12 As my statistics show, the result becomes blurred with larger figures. So it is very probable that if more material were collected it would no longer produce a similar result. We have therefore to be content with this apparently unique *lusus naturae,* though its uniqueness in no way prejudices the facts.

checking his probability calculations yet again, found that he had been deceived by the factor 5. The improbability of our results was again reduced, though without reaching a degree which one could have described as probable. *The errors all tend to exaggerate the results in a way favourable to astrology,* and add most suspiciously to the impression of an artificial or fraudulent arrangement of the facts, which was so mortifying to those concerned that they would probably have preferred to keep silent about it.

907 I know, however, from long experience of these things that spontaneous synchronistic phenomena draw the observer, by hook or by crook, into what is happening and occasionally make him an accessory to the deed. That is the danger inherent in all parapsychological experiments. The dependence of ESP on an emotional factor in the experimenter and subject is a case in point. I therefore consider it a scientific duty to give as complete an account as possible of the result and to show how not only the statistical material, but the psychic processes of the interested parties, were affected by the synchronistic arrangement. Although, warned by previous experience, I was cautious enough to submit my original account (in the Swiss edition) to four competent persons, among them two mathematicians, I allowed myself to be lulled into a sense of security too soon.

908 The corrections made here do not in any way alter the fact that the maximal frequencies lie with the three classical lunar aspects.

909 In order to assure myself of the chance nature of the result, I undertook one more statistical experiment. I broke up the original and fortuitous chronological order and the equally fortuitous division into three batches by mixing the first 150 marriages with the last 150, taking the latter in reverse order; that is to say, I put the first marriage on top of the last, and then the second on top of the last but one, and so on. Then I divided the 300 marriages into three batches of a hundred. The result was as follows:

	1st Batch	2nd Batch	3rd Batch
Maximum	No Aspects 11%	☉ ☌ ☌ 11% ☾ ☌ ☾ 11%	☾ ☌ *Asc.* 12%

910   The result of the first batch is amusing in so far as only fifteen of the 300 marriages have none of the fifty selected aspects in common. The second batch yields two maxima, of which the second again represents a classical conjunction. The third batch yields a maximum for ☾ ☌ *Asc.,* which we already know as the third "classical" conjunction. The total result shows that another chance arrangement of the marriages can easily produce a result that deviates from the earlier total, but still does not quite prevent the classical conjunctions from turning up.

*

911   The result of our experiment tallies with our experience of mantic procedures. One has the impression that these methods, and others like them, create favourable conditions for the occurrence of meaningful coincidences. It is quite true that the verification of synchronistic phenomena is a difficult and sometimes impossible task. Rhine's achievement in demonstrating, with the help of unexceptionable material, the coincidence of a psychic state with a corresponding objective process must therefore be rated all the higher. Despite the fact that the statistical method is in general highly unsuited to do justice to unusual events, Rhine's experiments have nevertheless withstood the ruinous influence of statistics. Their results must therefore be taken into account in any assessment of synchronistic phenomena.

912   In view of the levelling influence which the statistical method has on the quantitative determination of synchronicity, we must ask how it was that Rhine succeeded in obtaining positive results. I maintain that he would never have got the results he did if he had carried out his experiments with a single subject,[13] or only a few. He needed a constant renewal of interest, an emotion with its characteristic *abaissement mental,* which tips the scales in favour of the unconscious. Only in this way can space and time be relativized to a certain extent, thereby reducing the chances of a causal process. What then happens is a kind of *creatio ex nihilo,* an act of creation that is not causally explicable. The mantic procedures owe their effectiveness to

[13] By which I mean a subject chosen at random, and not one with specific gifts.

this same connection with emotionality: by touching an unconscious aptitude they stimulate interest, curiosity, expectation, hope, and fear, and consequently evoke a corresponding preponderance of the unconscious. The effective (numinous) agents in the unconscious are the archetypes. By far the greatest number of spontaneous synchronistic phenomena that I have had occasion to observe and analyse can easily be shown to have a direct connection with an archetype. This, in itself, is an irrepresentable, psychoid factor [14] of the collective unconscious. The latter cannot be localized, since either it is complete in principle in every individual or is found to be the same everywhere. You can never say with certainty whether what appears to be going on in the collective unconscious of a single individual is not also happening in other individuals or organisms or things or situations. When, for instance, the vision arose in Swedenborg's mind of a fire in Stockholm, there was a real fire raging there at the same time, without there being any demonstrable or even thinkable connection between the two.[15] I certainly would not like to undertake to prove the archetypal connection in this case. I would only point to the fact that in Swedenborg's biography there are certain things which throw a remarkable light on his psychic state. We must assume that there was a lowering of the threshold of consciousness which gave him access to "absolute knowledge." The fire in Stockholm was, in a sense, burning in him too. For the unconscious psyche space and time seem to be relative; that is to say, knowledge finds itself in a space-time continuum in which space is no longer space, nor time time. If, therefore, the unconscious should develop or maintain a potential in the direction of consciousness, it is then possible for parallel events to be perceived or "known."

913   Compared with Rhine's work the great disadvantage of my astrological statistics lies in the fact that the entire experiment was carried out on only one subject, myself. I did not experiment with a variety of subjects; rather, it was the varied material that challenged *my* interest. I was thus in the position of a subject who is at first enthusiastic, but afterwards cools off on

14 Cf. "On the Nature of the Psyche," pars. 417f.
15 This case is well authenticated. See report in Kant's *Dreams of a Spirit-Seer, Illustrated by Dreams of Metaphysics.*

becoming habituated to the ESP experiment. The results therefore deteriorated with the growing number of experiments, which in this case corresponded to the exposition of the material in batches, so that the accumulation of larger numbers only blurred the "favourable" initial result. Equally my final experiment showed that the discarding of the original order and the division of the horoscopes into arbitrary batches produce, as might be expected, a different picture, though its significance is not altogether clear.

914   Rhine's rules are to be recommended wherever (as in medicine) very large numbers are not involved. The interest and expectancy of the investigator might well be accompanied synchronistically by surprisingly favourable results to begin with, despite every precaution. These will be interpreted as "miracles" only by persons insufficiently acquainted with the statistical character of natural law.[16]

*

915   If—and it seems plausible—the meaningful coincidence or "cross-connection" of events cannot be explained causally, then the connecting principle must lie in the *equal significance* of parallel events; in other words, their *tertium comparationis* is *meaning*. We are so accustomed to regard meaning as a psychic process or content that it never enters our heads to suppose that it could also exist outside the psyche. But we do know at least enough about the psyche not to attribute to it any magical power, and still less can we attribute any magical power to the conscious mind. If, therefore, we entertain the hypothesis that one and the same (transcendental) meaning might manifest itself simultaneously in the human psyche and in the arrangement of an external and independent event, we at once come into conflict with the conventional scientific and epistemological views. We have to remind ourselves over and over again of the merely statistical validity of natural laws and of the effect of the statistical method in eliminating all unusual occurrences, if we want to lend an ear to such an hypothesis. The great difficulty is that we have absolutely no scientific means of proving the existence of an *objective* meaning which is not just a psychic

16 Cf. the interesting reflections of G. Spencer Brown: "De la recherche psychique considérée comme un test de la théorie des probabilités."

product. We are, however, driven to some such assumption if we are not to regress to a *magical causality* and ascribe to the psyche a power that far exceeds its empirical range of action. In that case we should have to suppose, if we don't want to let causality go, either that Swedenborg's unconscious staged the Stockholm fire, or conversely that the objective event activated in some quite inconceivable manner the corresponding images in Swedenborg's brain. In either case we come up against the unanswerable question of transmission discussed earlier. It is of course entirely a matter of subjective opinion which hypothesis is felt to make more sense. Nor does tradition help us much in choosing between magical causality and transcendental meaning, because on the one hand the primitive mentality has always explained synchronicity as magical causality right down to our own day, and on the other hand philosophy assumed a secret correspondence or meaningful connection between natural events until well into the eighteenth century. I prefer the latter hypothesis because it does not, like the first, conflict with the empirical concept of causality, and can count as a principle *sui generis*. That obliges us, not indeed to correct the principles of natural explanation as hitherto understood, but at least to add to their number, an operation which only the most cogent reasons could justify. I believe, however, that the hints I have given in the foregoing constitute an argument that needs thorough consideration. Psychology, of all the sciences, cannot in the long run afford to overlook such experiences. These things are too important for an understanding of the unconscious, quite apart from their philosophical implications.

APPENDIX TO CHAPTER 2

[The following notes have been compiled by the Editors on the basis of Professor Fierz's mathematical argument, of which he kindly furnished a précis. These represent his latest thoughts on the topic. These data are presented here for the benefit of readers with a special interest in mathematics or statistics who want to know how the figures in the text were arrived at.

Since an orbit of 8° was taken as the basis of Professor Jung's calculations for the estimation of conjunctions and oppositions (cf. par. 880), it follows that, for a particular relation between two heavenly bodies to be called a conjunction (e.g., sun ☌ moon), one of them must lie within an arc of 16°. (Since the only concern was to test the character of the distribution, an arc of 15° was taken for convenience.)

Now, all positions on a circle of 360° are equally probable. So the probability α that the heavenly body will lie on an arc of 15° is

$$\alpha = \frac{15}{360} = \frac{1}{24} \qquad (1)$$

This probability α holds for every aspect.

Let n be the number of particular aspects that will occur in N married pairs if the probability that it will occur in one married pair be α.

Applying the binomial distribution, we get:

$$W_n = \frac{N!}{n!(N-n)!}\, \alpha^n (1-\alpha)^{N-n} \qquad (2)$$

In order to obtain a numerical evaluation of W_n, (2) can be simplified. This results in an error, which, however, is not important. The simplification can be arrived at by replacing (2) by the Poisson distribution:

$$P_n = \frac{1}{n!}\, x^n \cdot e^{-x}$$

This approximation is valid if α may be regarded as very small in comparison with 1, while x is finite.

Upon the basis of these considerations the following numerical results can be arrived at:

(a) The probability of ☽ ☌ ☉, ☽ ☌ ☽, and ☽ ☌ *Asc.* turning up simultaneously is:

$$\alpha^3 = \left(\frac{1}{24}\right)^3 \sim \frac{1}{10,000}$$

(b) The probability P for the maximal figures in the three batches is:

1. 18 aspects in 180 married pairs, $P = 1 : 1,000$
2. 24 aspects in 220 married pairs, $P = 1 : 10,000$
3. 8 aspects in 83 married pairs, $P = 1 : 50$.

—EDITORS]

3. FORERUNNERS OF THE IDEA OF SYNCHRONICITY

916   The causality principle asserts that the connection between cause and effect is a necessary one. The synchronicity principle asserts that the terms of a meaningful coincidence are connected by *simultaneity* and *meaning*. So if we assume that the ESP experiments and numerous other observations are established facts, we must conclude that besides the connection between cause and effect there is another factor in nature which expresses itself in the arrangement of events and appears to us as meaning. Although meaning is an anthropomorphic interpretation it nevertheless forms the indispensable criterion of synchronicity. What that factor which appears to us as "meaning" may be in itself we have no possibility of knowing. As an hypothesis, however, it is not quite so impossible as may appear at first sight. We must remember that the rationalistic attitude of the West is not the only possible one and is not all-embracing, but is in many ways a prejudice and a bias that ought perhaps to be corrected. The very much older civilization of the Chinese has always thought differently from us in this respect, and we have to go back to Heraclitus if we want to find something similar in our civilization, at least where philosophy is concerned. Only in astrology, alchemy, and the mantic procedures do we find no differences of principle between our attitude and the Chinese. That is why alchemy developed along parallel lines in East and

West and why in both spheres it strove towards the same goal
with more or less identical ideas.[1]

917   In Chinese philosophy one of the oldest and most central
ideas is that of Tao, which the Jesuits translated as "God." But
that is correct only for the Western way of thinking. Other
translations, such as "Providence" and the like, are mere make-
shifts. Richard Wilhelm brilliantly interprets it as "meaning." [2]
The concept of Tao pervades the whole philosophical thought
of China. Causality occupies this paramount position with us,
but it acquired its importance only in the course of the last two
centuries, thanks to the levelling influence of the statistical
method on the one hand and the unparalleled success of the
natural sciences on the other, which brought the metaphysical
view of the world into disrepute.

918   Lao-tzu gives the following description of Tao in his cele-
brated *Tao Teh Ching:* [3]

> There is something formless yet complete
> That existed before heaven and earth.
>   How still! how empty!
> Dependent on nothing, unchanging,
> All pervading, unfailing.
> One may think of it as the mother of all things under heaven.
> I do not know its name,
> But I call it "Meaning."
> If I had to give it a name, I should call it "The Great."
> [Ch. XXV.]

919   Tao "covers the ten thousand things like a garment but does
not claim to be master over them"(Ch. XXXIV). Lao-tzu describes it as "Nothing," [4] by which he means, says Wilhelm,
only its "contrast with the world of reality." Lao-tzu describes
its nature as follows:

---

1 Cf. *Psychology and Alchemy*, par. 453, and "The Spirit Mercurius," par. 273.
Also the doctrine of *chên-yên* in Wei Po-yang ["Phil. Tree," pars. 432ff., and
Mysterium, pars. 490, 711n] and in Chuang-tzu.
2 Jung, "Commentary on *The Secret of the Golden Flower*," par. 28, and Wilhelm,
Chinesische Lebensweisheit.
3 [Quotations from Arthur Waley's *The Way and Its Power*, with occasional
slight changes to fit Wilhelm's reading.—TRANS.]
4 Tao is the contingent, which Andreas Speiser defines as "pure nothing" ("Über
die Freiheit").

We put thirty spokes together and call it a wheel;
But it is on the space where there is nothing that the utility of
the wheel depends.
We turn clay to make a vessel;
But it is on the space where there is nothing that the utility of
the vessel depends.
We pierce doors and windows to make a house;
And it is on these spaces where there is nothing that the utility of
the house depends.
Therefore just as we take advantage of what is, we should rec-
ognize the utility of what is not. [Ch. XI.]

920 "Nothing" is evidently "meaning" or "purpose," and it is
only called Nothing because it does not appear in the world of
the senses, but is only its organizer.[5] Lao-tzu says:

Because the eye gazes but can catch no glimpse of it,
It is called elusive.
Because the ear listens but cannot hear it,
It is called the rarefied.
Because the hand feels for it but cannot find it,
It is called the infinitesimal. . . .
These are called the shapeless shapes,
Forms without form,
Vague semblances.
Go towards them, and you can see no front;
Go after them, and you see no rear. [Ch. XIV.]

921 Wilhelm describes it as "a borderline conception lying at the
extreme edge of the world of appearances." In it, the opposites
"cancel out in non-discrimination," but are still potentially
present. "These seeds," he continues, "point to something that
corresponds firstly to *the visible,* i.e., something in the nature
of an image; secondly to *the audible,* i.e., something in the
nature of words; thirdly to *extension in space,* i.e., something
with a form. But these three things are not clearly distinguished
and definable, they are a non-spatial and non-temporal unity,
having no above and below or front and back." As the *Tao Teh
Ching* says:

---

5 Wilhelm, *Chinesische Lebensweisheit,* p. 15: "The relation between meaning
(Tao) and reality cannot be conceived under the category of cause and effect."

Incommensurable, impalpable,
Yet latent in it are forms;
Impalpable, incommensurable,
Yet within it are entities.
Shadowy it is and dim. [Ch. XXI.]

922   Reality, thinks Wilhelm, is conceptually knowable because
according to the Chinese view there is in all things a latent
"rationality." [6] This is the basic idea underlying meaningful
coincidence: it is possible because both sides have the same
meaning. Where meaning prevails, order results:

Tao is eternal, but has no name;
The Uncarved Block, though seemingly of small account,
Is greater than anything under heaven.
If the kings and barons would but possess themselves of it,
The ten thousand creatures would flock to do them homage;
Heaven and earth would conspire
To send Sweet Dew;
Without law or compulsion men would dwell in harmony.
[Ch. XXXII.]

Tao never does;
Yet through it all things are done. [Ch. XXXVII.]

Heaven's net is wide;
Coarse are the meshes, yet nothing slips through. [Ch. LXXIII.]

923   Chuang-tzu (a contemporary of Plato's) says of the psychological premises on which Tao is based: "The state in which
ego and non-ego are no longer opposed is called the pivot of
Tao." [7] It sounds almost like a criticism of our scientific view of
the world when he remarks that "Tao is obscured when you
fix your eye on little segments of existence only," [8] or "Limita-
tions are not originally grounded in the meaning of life. Originally words had no fixed meanings. Differences only arose
through looking at things subjectively." [9] The sages of old, says
Chuang-tzu, "took as their starting-point a state when the
existence of things had not yet begun. That is indeed the ex-

6 Ibid., p. 19.
7 Das wahre Buch vom südlichen Blütenland, trans. by R. Wilhelm, II, 3.
8 Ibid., II, 3.   9 II, 7.

treme limit beyond which you cannot go. The next assumption was that though things existed they had not yet begun to be separated. The next, that though things were separated in a sense, affirmation and negation had not yet begun. When affirmation and negation came into being, Tao faded. After Tao faded, then came one-sided attachments." [10] "Outward hearing should not penetrate further than the ear; the intellect should not seek to lead a separate existence, thus the soul can become empty and absorb the whole world. It is Tao that fills this emptiness." If you have insight, says Chuang-tzu, "you use your inner eye, your inner ear, to pierce to the heart of things, and have no need of intellectual knowledge." [11] This is obviously an allusion to the absolute knowledge of the unconscious, and to the presence in the microcosm of macrocosmic events.

924   This Taoistic view is typical of Chinese thinking. It is, whenever possible, *a thinking in terms of the whole,* a point also brought out by Marcel Granet,[12] the eminent authority on Chinese psychology. This peculiarity can be seen in ordinary conversation with the Chinese: what seems to us a perfectly straightforward, precise question about some detail evokes from the Chinese thinker an unexpectedly elaborate answer, as though one had asked him for a blade of grass and got a whole meadow in return. With us details are important for their own sakes; for the Oriental mind they always complete a total picture. In this totality, as in primitive or in our own medieval, pre-scientific psychology (still very much alive!), are included things which seem to be connected with one another only "by chance," by a coincidence whose meaningfulness appears altogether arbitrary. This is where the theory of *correspondentia* [13] comes in, which was propounded by the natural philosophers of the Middle Ages, and particularly the classical idea of the *sympathy of all things.*[14] Hippocrates says:

10 II, 5.   11 IV, 1.

12 *La Pensée chinoise;* also Lily Abegg, *The Mind of East Asia.* The latter gives an excellent account of the synchronistic mentality of the Chinese.

13 Professor W. Pauli kindly calls my attention to the fact that Niels Bohr used "correspondence" as a mediating term between the representation of the discontinuum (particle) and the continuum (wave). Originally (1913–18) he called it the "principle of correspondence," but later (1927) it was formulated as the "argument of correspondence."   14 "συμπάθεια τῶν ὅλων."

There is one common flow, one common breathing, all things are in sympathy. The whole organism and each one of its parts are working in conjunction for the same purpose . . . the great principle extends to the extremest part, and from the extremest part it returns to the great principle, to the one nature, being and not-being.[15]

The universal principle is found even in the smallest particle, which therefore corresponds to the whole.

925   In this connection there is an interesting idea in Philo (25 B.C.–A.D. 42):

God, being minded to unite in intimate and loving fellowship the beginning and end of created things, made heaven the beginning and man the end, the one the most perfect of imperishable objects of sense, the other the noblest of things earthborn and perishable, being, in very truth, a miniature heaven. He bears about within himself, like holy images, endowments of nature that correspond to the constellations. . . . For since the corruptible and the incorruptible are by nature contrary the one to the other, God assigned the fairest of each sort to the beginning and the end, heaven (as I have said) to the beginning, and man to the end.[16]

926   Here the great principle [17] or beginning, heaven, is infused into man the microcosm, who reflects the star-like natures and thus, as the smallest part and end of the work of Creation, contains the whole.

927   According to Theophrastus (371–288 B.C.) the suprasensuous and the sensuous are joined by a bond of community. This bond cannot be mathematics, so must presumably be God.[18] Similarly in Plotinus the individual souls born of the one World Soul are related to one another by sympathy or antipathy, regardless of distance.[19] Similar views are to be found in Pico della Mirandola:

15 De alimento, a tract ascribed to Hippocrates. (Trans. by John Precope in Hippocrates on Diet and Hygiene, p. 174, modified.) "Σύρροια μία, συμπνοία μία, πάντα συμπαθέα κατὰ μὲν οὐλομελίην πάντα κατὰ μέρος δὲ τὰ ἐν ἑκάστῳ μέρει μερέα πρὸς τὸ ἔργον . . . ἀρχὴ μεγάλη ἐς ἔσχατον μέρος ἀφικνέεται, ἐξ ἐσχάτου μέρεος εἰς ἀρχὴν μεγάλην ἀφικνέεται, μία φύσις εἶναι καὶ μὴ εἶναι."
16 De opificio mundi, 82 (trans. by F. H. Colson and G. H. Whitaker, I, p. 67).
17 "ἀρχὴ μεγάλη"
18 Eduard Zeller, Die Philosophie der Griechen, II, part ii, p. 654.
19 Enneads, IV, 3, 8 and 4, 32 (in A. C. H. Drews, Plotin und der Untergang der antiken Weltanschauung, p. 179).

Firstly there is the unity in things whereby each thing is at one with itself, consists of itself, and coheres with itself. Secondly there is the unity whereby one creature is united with the others and all parts of the world constitute one world. The third and most important (unity) is that whereby the whole universe is one with its Creator, as an army with its commander.[20]

By this threefold unity Pico means a simple unity which, like the Trinity, has three aspects; "a unity distinguished by a three-fold character, yet in such a way as not to depart from the simplicity of unity." [21] For him the world is *one* being, a visible God, in which everything is naturally arranged from the very beginning like the parts of a living organism. The world appears as the *corpus mysticum* of God, just as the Church is the *corpus mysticum* of Christ, or as a well-disciplined army can be called a sword in the hand of the commander. The view that all things are arranged according to God's will is one that leaves little room for causality. Just as in a living body the different parts work in harmony and are meaningfully adjusted to one another, so events in the world stand in a meaningful relationship which cannot be derived from any immanent causality. The reason for this is that in either case the behaviour of the parts depends on a central control which is supraordinate to them.

928   In his treatise *De hominis dignitate* Pico says: "The Father implanted in man at birth seeds of all kinds and the germs of original life." [22] Just as God is the "copula" of the world, so, within the created world, is man. "Let us make man in our image, who is not a fourth world or anything like a new nature, but is rather the fusion and synthesis of three worlds (the supra-celestial, the celestial, and the sublunary)." [23] In body and spirit

---

20 *Heptaplus*, VI, prooem., in *Opera omnia*, pp. 40f. ("Est enim primum ea in rebus unitas, qua unumquodque sibi est unum sibique constat atque cohaeret. Est ea secundo, per quam altera alteri creatura unitur, et per quam demum omnes mundi partes unus sunt mundus. Tertia atque omnium principalissima est, qua totum universum cum suo opifice quasi exercitus cum suo duce est unum.")
21 "unitas ita ternario distincta, ut ab unitatis simplicitate non discedat."
22 *Opera omnia*, p. 315. ("Nascenti homini omnifaria semina et origenae vitae germina indidit pater.")
23 *Heptaplus*, V, vi, in ibid., p. 38. ("Faciamus hominem ad imaginem nostram, qui non tam quartus est mundus, quasi nova aliqua natura, quam trium (mundus supercoelestis, coelestis, sublunaris) complexus et colligatio."

man is "the little God of the world," the microcosm.[24] Like God, therefore, man is a centre of events, and all things revolve about him.[25] This thought, so utterly strange to the modern mind, dominated man's picture of the world until a few generations ago, when natural science proved man's subordination to nature and his extreme dependence on causes. The idea of a correlation between events and meaning (now assigned exclusively to man) was banished to such a remote and benighted region that the intellect lost track of it altogether. Schopenhauer remembered it somewhat belatedly after it had formed one of the chief items in Leibniz's scientific explanations.

929   By virtue of his microcosmic nature man is a son of the firmament or macrocosm. "I am a star travelling together with you," the initiate confesses in the Mithraic liturgy.[26] In alchemy the microcosmos has the same significance as the *rotundum*, a favourite symbol since the time of Zosimos of Panopolis, which was also known as the Monad.

930   The idea that the inner and outer man together form the whole, the οὐλομελίη of Hippocrates, a microcosm or smallest part wherein the "great principle" is undividedly present, also characterizes the thought of Agrippa von Nettesheim. He says:

> It is the unanimous consent of all Platonists, that as in the archetypal World, all things are in all; so also in this corporeal world, all things are in all, albeit in different ways, according to the receptive nature of each. Thus the Elements are not only in these inferiour bodies, but also in the Heavens, in Stars, in Divels, in Angels, and lastly in God, the maker, and archetype of all things.[27]

24 "God . . . placed man in the centre [of the world] after his image and the similitude of forms" ("Deus . . . hominem in medio [mundi] statuit ad imaginem suam et similitudinem formarum").

25 Pico's doctrine is a typical example of the medieval correspondence theory. A good account of cosmological and astrological correspondence is to be found in Alfons Rosenberg, *Zeichen am Himmel: Das Weltbild der Astrologie.*

26 Albrecht Dieterich, *Eine Mithrasliturgie*, p. 9.

27 Henricus Cornelius Agrippa von Nettesheim, *De occulta philosophia Libri tres*, I, viii, p. 12. Trans. by "J. F." as *Three Books of Occult Philosophy* (1651 edn.), p. 20; republished under the editorship of W. F. Whitehead, p. 55. [Quotations from the J. F. translation have been slightly modified.—TRANS.] ("Est Platonicorum omnium unanimis sententia quemadmodum in archetypo mundo omnia sunt in omnibus, ita etiam in hoc corporeo mundo, omnia in omnibus esse, modis tamen diversis, pro natura videlicet suscipientium: sic et elementa non solum sunt in istis inferioribus, sed in coelis, in stellis, in daemonibus, in angelis, in ipso denique omnium opifice et archetypo.")

The ancients had said: "All things are full of gods." [28] These gods were "divine powers which are diffused in things." [29] Zoroaster had called them "divine allurements," [30] and Synesius "symbolic inticements." [31] This latter interpretation comes very close indeed to the idea of archetypal projections in modern psychology, although from the time of Synesius until quite recently there was no epistemological criticism, let alone the newest form of it, namely psychological criticism. Agrippa shares with the Platonists the view that "there is in the lower beings a certain virtue through which they agree in large measure with the higher," and that as a result the animals are connected with the "divine bodies" (i.e., the stars) and exert an influence on them.[32] Here he quotes Virgil: "I for my part do not believe that they [the rooks] are endowed with divine spirit or with a foreknowledge of things greater than the oracle." [33]

931   Agrippa is thus suggesting that there is an inborn "knowledge" or "perception" in living organisms, an idea which recurs in our own day in Hans Driesch.[34] Whether we like it or not, we find ourselves in this embarrassing position as soon as we begin seriously to reflect on the teleological processes in biology or to investigate the compensatory function of the unconscious, not to speak of trying to explain the phenomenon of synchronicity. Final causes, twist them how we will, postulate a *foreknowledge of some kind*. It is certainly not a knowledge that could be connected with the ego, and hence not a conscious knowledge as we know it, but rather a self-subsistent "unconscious" knowledge which I would prefer to call "absolute knowledge." It is not cognition but, as Leibniz so excellently calls it,

---

28 "Omna plena diis esse."   29 "virtutes divinae in rebus diffusae"
30 "divinae illices"
31 "symbolicae illecebrae." [In J. F. original edn., p. 32; Whitehead edn., p. 69.— Trans.] Agrippa is basing himself here on the Marsilio Ficino translation (*Auctores Platonici*, II, vº). In Synesius (*Opuscula*, ed. by Nicolaus Terzaghi, p. 148), the text of Περὶ ἐνυπνίων III B has τὸ θελγόμενον, from θέλγειν, "to excite, charm, enchant."
32 *De occulta philosophia*, I, iv, p. 69. (J. F. edn., p. 117; Whitehead edn., p. 169.) Similarly in Paracelsus.
33 "Haud equidem credo, quia sit divinius illis
     Ingenium aut rerum fato prudentia maior."
                              —*Georgics*, I, 415f.
34 *Die "Seele" als elementarer Naturfaktor*, pp. 80, 82.

a "perceiving" which consists—or to be more cautious, seems to consist—of images, of subjectless "simulacra." These postulated images are presumably the same as my archetypes, which can be shown to be formal factors in spontaneous fantasy products. Expressed in modern language, the microcosm which contains "the images of all creation" would be the collective unconscious.[35] By the *spiritus mundi*, the *ligamentum animae et corporis*, the *quinta essentia*,[36] which he shares with the alchemists, Agrippa probably means what we would call the unconscious. The spirit that "penetrates all things," or shapes all things, is the World Soul: "The soul of the world therefore is a certain only thing, filling all things, bestowing all things, binding, and knitting together all things, that it might make one frame of the world. . . ." [37] Those things in which this spirit is particularly powerful therefore have a tendency to "beget their like," [38] in other words, to produce correspondences or meaningful coincidences.[39] Agrippa gives a long list of these correspondences, based on the numbers 1 to 12.[40] A similar but more alchemical table of correspondences can be found in a treatise of Aegidius de Vadis.[41] Of these I would only mention the *scala unitatis*, because it is especially interesting from the point of

35 Cf. supra, "On the Nature of the Psyche," pars. 392f.

36 Agrippa says of this (op. cit., I, xiv, p. 29; J. F. edn., p. 33; Whitehead edn., p. 70): "That which we call the quintessence: because it is not from the four Elements, but a certain fifth thing, having its being above, and besides them." ("Quoddam quintum super illa [elementa] aut praeter illa subsistens.")

37 II, lvii, p. 203 (J. F. edn., p. 331): "Est itaque anima mundi, vita quaedam unica omnia replens, omnia perfundens, omnia colligens et connectens, ut unam reddat totius mundi machinam. . . ."

38 Ibid.: ". . . potentius perfectiusque agunt, tum etiam promptius generant sibi simile."

39 The zoologist A. C. Hardy reaches similar conclusions: "Perhaps our ideas on evolution may be altered if something akin to telepathy—unconscious no doubt— were found to be a factor in moulding the patterns of behaviour among members of a species. If there was such a non-conscious group-behaviour plan, distributed between, and linking, the individuals of the race, we might find ourselves coming back to something like those ideas of subconscious racial memory of Samuel Butler, but on a group rather than an individual basis." "The Scientific Evidence for Extra-Sensory Perception," in *Discovery*, X, 328, quoted by Soal, q.v.

40 Op. cit., II, iv–xiv.

41 "Dialogus inter naturam et filium philosophiae." *Theatrum chemicum*, II (1602), p. 123.

view of the history of symbols: "Yod [the first letter of the tetragrammaton, the divine▾ name]—anima mundi—sol—lapis philosophorum—cor—Lucifer." [42] I must content myself with saying that this is an attempt to set up a hierarchy of archetypes, and that tendencies in this direction can be shown to exist in the unconscious. [43]

932   Agrippa was an older contemporary of Theophrastus Paracelsus and is known to have had a considerable influence on him. [44] So it is not surprising if the thinking of Paracelsus proves to be steeped in the idea of correspondence. He says:

> If a man will be a philosopher without going astray, he must lay the foundations of his philosophy by making heaven and earth a microcosm, and not be wrong by a hair's breadth. Therefore he who will lay the foundations of medicine must also guard against the slightest error, and must make from the microcosm the revolution of heaven and earth, so that the philosopher does not find anything in heaven and earth which he does not also find in man, and the physician does not find anything in man which heaven and earth do not have. And these two differ only in outward form, and yet the form on both sides is understood as pertaining to one thing. [45]

The *Paragranum* [46] has some pointed psychological remarks to make about physicians:

> For this reason, [we assume] not four, but one arcanum, which is, however, four-square, like a tower facing the four winds. And as little as a tower may lack a corner, so little may the physician lack one of the parts. . . . At the same [time he] knows how the world is symbolized [by] an egg in its shell, and how a chick with all its substance lies hidden within it. Thus everything in the world and in man must lie hidden in the physician. And just as the hens, by their brooding, transform the world prefigured in the shell into a chick, so Alchemy brings to maturity the philosophical arcana lying in the

---

42 Cited in Agrippa, op. cit., II, iv, p. 104 (J. F. edn., p. 176).

43 Cf. Aniela Jaffé, "Bilder und Symbole aus E. T. A. Hoffmann's Märchen 'Der goldene Topf,' " and Marie-Louise von Franz, "Die Passio Perpetuae."

44 Cf. *Alchemical Studies*, index, s.v. "Agrippa."

45 *Das Buch Paragranum*, ed. by Franz Strunz, pp. 35f. Much the same in *Labyrinthus medicorum*, in the *Sämtliche Werke*, ed. Sudhoff, XI, pp. 204ff.

46 Strunz edn., p. 34.

physician. . . . Herein lies the error of those who do not understand the physician aright.[47]

What this means for alchemy I have shown in some detail in my
Psychology and Alchemy.

933   Johannes Kepler thought in much the same way. He says in
his *Tertius interveniens* (1610): [48]

> This [viz., a geometrical principle underlying the physical world] is
> also, according to the doctrine of Aristotle, the strongest tie that
> links the lower world to the heavens and unifies it therewith so that
> all its forms are governed from on high; for in this lower world, that
> is to say the globe of the earth, there is inherent a spiritual nature,
> capable of *Geometria*, which *ex instinctu creatoris, sine ratio-
> cinatione* comes to life and stimulates itself into a use of its forces
> through the geometrical and harmonious combination of the heav-
> enly rays of light. Whether all plants and animals as well as the
> globe of the earth have this faculty in themselves I cannot say. But
> it is not an unbelievable thing. . . . For, in all these things [e.g., in
> the fact that flowers have a definite colour, form, and number of
> petals] there is at work the *instinctus divinus, rationis particeps,* and
> not at all man's own intelligence. That man, too, through his soul
> and its lower faculties, has a like affinity to the heavens as has the
> soil of the earth can be tested and proven in many ways.[49]

934   Concerning the astrological "Character," i.e., astrological
synchronicity, Kepler says:

> This *Character* is received, not into the body, which is much too
> inappropriate for this, but into the soul's own nature, which behaves
> like a point (for which reason it can also be transformed into the
> point of the *confluxus radiorum*). This [nature of the soul] not only
> partakes of their reason (on account of which we human beings are
> called reasonable above other living creatures) but also has another,
> innate reason [enabling it] to apprehend instantaneously, without
> long learning, the *Geometriam* in the *radiis* as well as in the *vocibus*,
> that is to say, in *Musica*.[50]

[47] Similar ideas in Jakob Böhme, *The Signature of All Things*, trans. by John
Ellistone, p. 10: "Man has indeed the forms of all the three worlds in him, for
he is a complete image of God, or of the Being of all beings. . . ." (*Signatura
rerum*, I, 7.)
[48] *Opera omnia*, ed. by C. Frisch, I, pp. 605ff.
[49] Ibid., No. 64.   [50] No. 65.

Thirdly, another marvellous thing is that the nature which receives this *Characterem* also induces a certain correspondence *in constellationibus coelestibus* in its relatives. When a mother is great with child and the natural time of delivery is near, nature selects for the birth a day and hour which correspond, on account of the heavens [scil., from an astrological point of view], to the nativity of the mother's brother or father, and this *non qualitative, sed astronomice et quantitative.*[51]

Fourthly, so well does each nature know not only its *characterem coelestem* but also the celestial *configurationes* and courses of every day that, whenever a planet moves *de praesenti* into its *characteris ascendentem* or *loca praecipua*, especially into the *Natalitia*,[52] it responds to this and is affected and stimulated thereby in various ways.[53]

935   Kepler supposes that the secret of the marvellous correspondence is to be found in the *earth*, because the earth is animated by an *anima telluris*, for whose existence he adduces a number of proofs. Among these are: the constant temperature below the surface of the earth; the peculiar power of the earth-soul to produce metals, minerals, and fossils, namely the *facultas formatrix*, which is similar to that of the womb and can bring forth in the bowels of the earth shapes that are otherwise found only outside —ships, fishes, kings, popes, monks, soldiers, etc.; [54] further the practice of geometry, for it produces the five geometrical bodies and the six-cornered figures in crystals. The *anima telluris* has all this from an original impulse, independent of the reflection and ratiocination of man.[55]

936   The seat of astrological synchronicity is not in the planets but in the earth; [56] not in matter, but in the *anima telluris.*

51 No. 67.

52 ["in die Natalitia" = "into those [positions presiding] at birth," if "in die" is construed as German. The *Gesammelte Werke*, ed. by M. Caspar and F. Hammer, IV, p. 211, has "in die Natalitio" = "in the day of birth," the words "in die" being construed as Latin.—TRANS.]   53 No. 68.

54 See the dreams mentioned below.

55 Kepler, *Opera*, ed. by Frisch, V, p. 254; cf. also II, pp. 270f. and VI, pp. 178f. ". . . formatrix facultas est in visceribus terrae, quae feminae praegnantis more occursantes foris res humanas veluti eas videret, in fissibilibus lapidibus exprimit, ut militum, monachorum, pontificum, regum et quidquid in ore hominum est. . . ."

56 ". . . quod scl. principatus causae in terra sedeat, non in planetis ipsis." Ibid., II, p. 642.

Therefore every kind of natural or living power in bodies has a certain "divine similitude." [57]

*

937   Such was the intellectual background when Gottfried Wilhelm von Leibniz (1646–1716) appeared with his idea of *pre-established harmony*, that is, an absolute synchronism of psychic and physical events. This theory finally petered out in the concept of "psychophysical parallelism." Leibniz's pre-established harmony and the above-mentioned idea of Schopenhauer's, that the unity of the primal cause produces a simultaneity and inter-relationship of events not in themselves causally connected, are at bottom only a repetition of the old peripatetic view, with a modern deterministic colouring in the case of Schopenhauer and a partial replacement of causality by an antecedent order in the case of Leibniz. For him God is the creator of order. He compares soul and body to two synchronized clocks [58] and uses

[57] ". . . ut omne genus naturalium vel animalium facultatum in corporibus Dei quandam gerat similitudinem." Ibid. I am indebted to Dr. Liliane Frey-Rohn and Dr. Marie-Louise von Franz for this reference to Kepler.

[58] G. W. Leibniz, "Second Explanation of the System of the Communication between Substances" (*The Philosophical Works of Leibniz*, trans. by. G. M. Duncan, pp. 90–91): "From the beginning God has made each of these two substances of such a nature that merely by following its own peculiar laws, received with its being, it nevertheless accords with the other, just as if there were a mutual influence or as if God always put his hand thereto in addition to his general co-operation."

As Professor Pauli has kindly pointed out, it is possible that Leibniz took his idea of the synchronized clocks from the Flemish philosopher Arnold Geulincx (1625–99). In his *Metaphysica vera*, Part III, there is a note to "Octava scientia" (p. 195), which says (p. 296): ". . . horologium voluntatis nostrae quadret cum horologium motus in corpore" (the clock of our will is synchronized with the clock of our physical movement). Another note (p. 297) explains: "Voluntas nostra nullum habet influxum, causalitatem, determinationem aut efficaciam quamcunque in motum . . . cum cogitationes nostras bene excutimus, nullam apud nos invenimus ideam seu notionem determinationis. . . . Restat igitur Deus solus primus motor et solus motor, quia et ita motum ordinat atque disponit et ita simul voluntati nostrae licet libere moderatur, ut eodem temporis momento conspiret et voluntas nostra ad projiciendum v.g. pedes inter ambulandum, et simul ipsa illa pedum projectio seu ambulatio." (Our will has no influence, no causative or determinative power, and no effect of any kind on our movement. . . . If we examine our thoughts carefully, we find in ourselves no idea or concept of determination. . . . There remains, therefore, only God as the prime

the same simile to express the relations of the monads or entelechies with one another. Although the monads cannot influence one another directly because, as he says, they "have no windows" [59] (relative abolition of causality!), they are so constituted that they are always in accord without having knowledge of one another. He conceives each monad to be a "little world" or "active indivisible mirror." [60] Not only is man a microcosm enclosing the whole in himself, but every entelechy or monad is in effect such a microcosm. Each "simple substance" has connections "which express all the others." It is "a perpetual living mirror of the universe." [61] He calls the monads of living organisms "souls": "the soul follows its own laws, and the body its own likewise, and they accord by virtue of the harmony pre-established among all substances, since they are all representations of one and the same universe." [62] This clearly expresses the idea that man is a microcosm. "Souls in general," says Leibniz, "are the living mirrors or images of the universe of created things." He distinguishes between minds on the one hand, which are "images of the Divinity . . . capable of knowing the system of the universe, and of imitating something of it by architectonic patterns, each mind being as it were a little

---

mover and only mover, because he arranges and orders movement and freely co-ordinates it with our will, so that our will wishes simultaneously to throw the feet forward into walking, and simultaneously the forward movement and the walking take place.) A note to "Nona scientia" adds (p. 298): "Mens nostra . . . penitus independens est ab illo (scl. corpore) . . . omnia quae de corpore scimus jam praevie quasi ante nostram cognitionem esse in corpore. Ut illa quodam modo nos in corpore legamus, non vero inscribamus, quod Deo proprium est." (Our mind . . . is totally independent of the body . . . everything we know about the body is already in the body, before our thought. So that we can, as it were, read ourselves in our body, but not imprint ourselves on it. Only God can do that.) This idea anticipates Leibniz' clock comparison.

59 *Monadology*, § 7: "Monads have no windows, by which anything could come in or go out. . . . Thus neither substance nor accident can enter a monad from without."

60 Rejoinder to the remarks in Bayle's Dictionary, from the *Kleinere philosophische Schriften*, XI, p. 105.

61 *Monadology*, § 56 (Morris edn., p. 12): "Now this connection or adaptation of all created things with each, and of each with all the rest, means that each simple substance has relations which express all the others, and that consequently it is a perpetual living mirror of the universe." 62 Ibid., § 78 (p. 17).

divinity in its own department," [63] and bodies on the other hand, which "act according to the laws of efficient causes by motions," while the souls act "according to the laws of final causes by appetitions, ends, and means." [64] In the monad or soul alterations take place whose cause is the "appetition." [65] "The passing state, which involves and represents a plurality within the unity or simple substance, is nothing other than what is called perception," says Leibniz.[66] Perception is the "inner state of the monad representing external things," and it must be distinguished from conscious apperception. "For perception is unconscious." [67] Herein lay the great mistake of the Cartesians, "that they took no account of perceptions which are not apperceived." [68] The perceptive faculty of the monad corresponds to the *knowledge,* and its appetitive faculty to the *will,* that is in God.[69]

938   It is clear from these quotations that besides the causal connection Leibniz postulates a complete pre-established parallelism of events both inside and outside the monad. The synchronicity principle thus becomes the absolute rule in all cases where an inner event occurs simultaneously with an outside one. As against this, however, it must be borne in mind that the synchronistic phenomena which can be verified empirically, far from constituting a rule, are so exceptional that most people doubt their existence. They certainly occur much more frequently in reality than one thinks or can prove, but we still do not know whether they occur so frequently and so regularly in any field of experience that we could speak of them as conforming to law.[70] We only know that there must be an under-

---

[63] § 83 (p. 18); cf. *Theodicy,* § 147 (trans. by E. M. Huggard, pp. 215f.).
[64] *Monadology,* § 79 (Morris edn., p. 17).   [65] Ibid., § 15 (p. 5).
[66] § 14 (pp. 4f.).
[67] *Principles of Nature and of Grace, Founded on Reason,* § 4 (Morris edn., p. 22).
[68] *Monadology,* § 14 (p. 5). Cf. also Dr. Marie-Louise von Franz's paper on the dream of Descartes in *Zeitlose Dokumente der Seele.*
[69] *Monadology,* § 48 (p. 11); *Theodicy,* § 149.
[70] I must again stress the possibility that the relation between body and soul may yet be understood as a synchronistic one. Should this conjecture ever be proved, my present view that synchronicity is a relatively rare phenomenon would have to be corrected. Cf. C. A. Meier's observations in *Zeitgemässe Probleme der Traumforschung,* p. 22.

lying principle which might possibly explain all such (related) phenomena.

939 The primitive as well as the classical and medieval views of nature postulate the existence of some such principle alongside causality. Even in Leibniz, causality is neither the only view nor the predominant one. Then, in the course of the eighteenth century, it became the exclusive principle of natural science. With the rise of the physical sciences in the nineteenth century the correspondence theory vanished completely from the surface, and the magical world of earlier ages seemed to have disappeared once and for all until, towards the end of the century, the founders of the Society for Psychical Research indirectly opened up the whole question again through their investigation of telepathic phenomena.

940 The medieval attitude of mind I have described above underlies all the magical and mantic procedures which have played an important part in man's life since the remotest times. The medieval mind would regard Rhine's laboratory-arranged experiments as magical performances, whose effect for this reason would not seem so very astonishing. It was interpreted as a "transmission of energy," which is still commonly the case today, although, as I have said, it is not possible to form any empirically verifiable conception of the transmitting medium.

941 I need hardly point out that for the primitive mind synchronicity is a self-evident fact; consequently at this stage there is no such thing as chance. No accident, no illness, no death is ever fortuitous or attributable to "natural" causes. Everything is somehow due to magical influence. The crocodile that catches a man while he is bathing has been sent by a magician; illness is caused by some spirit or other; the snake that was seen by the grave of somebody's mother is obviously her soul; etc. On the primitive level, of course, synchronicity does not appear as an idea by itself, but as "magical" causality. This is an early form of our classical idea of causality, while the development of Chinese philosophy produced from the significance of the magical the "concept" of Tao, of meaningful coincidence, but no causality-based science.

942 Synchronicity postulates a meaning which is *a priori* in relation to human consciousness and apparently exists outside

man.[71] Such an assumption is found above all in the philosophy of Plato, which takes for granted the existence of transcendental images or models of empirical things, the εἴδη (forms, species), whose reflections (εἴδωλα) we see in the phenomenal world. This assumption not only presented no difficulty to earlier centuries but was on the contrary perfectly self-evident. The idea of an *a priori* meaning may also be found in the older mathematics, as in the mathematician Jacobi's paraphrase of Schiller's poem "Archimedes and His Pupil." He praises the calculation of the orbit of Uranus and closes with the lines:

> What you behold in the cosmos is only the light of God's glory;
> In the Olympian host Number eternally reigns.

943   The great mathematician Gauss is the putative author of the saying: "God arithmetizes." [72]

944   The idea of synchronicity and of a self-subsistent meaning, which forms the basis of classical Chinese thinking and of the naïve views of the Middle Ages, seems to us an archaic assumption that ought at all costs to be avoided. Though the West has done everything possible to discard this antiquated hypothesis, it has not quite succeeded. Certain mantic procedures seem to have died out, but astrology, which in our own day has attained an eminence never known before, remains very much alive. Nor has the determinism of a scientific epoch been able to extinguish altogether the persuasive power of the synchronicity principle. For in the last resort it is not so much a question of superstition as of a truth which remained hidden for so long only because it had less to do with the physical side of events than with their psychic aspects. It was modern psychology and parapsychology which proved that causality does not explain a certain class of

[71] In view of the possibility that synchronicity is not only a psychophysical phenomenon but might also occur without the participation of the human psyche, I should like to point out that in this case we should have to speak not of *meaning* but of equivalence or conformity.

[72] "ὁ θεὸς ἀριθμητίζει." But in a letter of 1830 Gauss says: "We must in all humility admit that if number is *merely* a product of our mind, space has a reality outside our mind." (Leopold Kronecker, *Über den Zahlenbegriff*, in his *Werke*, III, p. 252.) Hermann Weyl likewise takes number as a product of reason. ("Wissenschaft als symbolische Konstruktion des Menschen," p. 375). Markus Fierz, on the other hand, inclines more to the Platonic idea. ("Zur physikalischen Erkenntnis," p. 434.)

events and that in this case we have to consider a formal factor, namely synchronicity, as a principle of explanation.

945 For those who are interested in psychology I should like to mention here that the peculiar idea of a self-subsistent meaning is suggested in dreams. Once when this idea was being discussed in my circle somebody remarked: "The geometrical square does not occur in nature except in crystals." A lady who had been present had the following dream that night: *In the garden there was a large sandpit in which layers of rubbish had been deposited. In one of these layers she discovered thin, slaty plates of green serpentine. One of them had black squares on it, arranged concentrically. The black was not painted on, but was ingrained in the stone, like the markings in an agate. Similar marks were found on two or three other plates, which Mr. A (a slight acquaintance) then took away from her.*[73] Another dream-motif of the same kind is the following: *The dreamer was in a wild mountain region where he found contiguous layers of triassic rock. He loosened the slabs and discovered to his boundless astonishment that they had human heads on them in low relief.* This dream was repeated several times at long intervals.[74] Another time the dreamer *was travelling through the Siberian tundra and found an animal he had long been looking for. It was a more than lifesize cock, made of what looked like thin, colourless glass. But it was alive and had just sprung by chance from a microscopic unicellular organism which had the power to turn into all sorts of animals (not otherwise found in the tundra) or even into objects of human use, of whatever size. The next moment each of these chance forms vanished without trace.* Here is another dream of the same type: *The dreamer was walking in a wooded mountain region. At the top of a steep slope he came to a ridge of rock honeycombed with holes, and there he found a little brown man of the same colour as the iron oxide with which the rock was coated.*[75] *The little man was busily*

---

[73] According to the rules of dream interpretation this Mr. A would represent the animus, who, as a personification of the unconscious, takes back the designs because the conscious mind has no use for them and regards them only as *lusus naturae.*

[74] The recurrence of the dream expresses the persistent attempt of the unconscious to bring the dream content before the conscious mind.

[75] An Anthroparion or "metallic man."

engaged in hollowing out a cave, at the back of which a cluster of columns could be seen in the living rock. On the top of each column was a dark brown human head with large eyes, carved with great care out of some very hard stone, like lignite. The little man freed this formation from the amorphous conglomerate surrounding it. The dreamer could hardly believe his eyes at first, but then had to admit that the columns were continued far back into the living rock and must therefore have come into existence without the help of man. He reflected that the rock was at least half a million years old and that the artefact could not possibly have been made by human hands.[76]

946   These dreams seem to point to the presence of a formal factor in nature. They describe not just a *lusus naturae,* but the meaningful coincidence of an absolutely natural product with a human idea apparently independent of it. This is what the dreams are obviously saying,[77] and what they are trying to bring nearer to consciousness through repetition.

[76] Cf. Kepler's ideas quoted above.

[77] Those who find the dreams unintelligible will probably suspect them of harbouring quite a different meaning which is more in accord with their preconceived opinions. One can indulge in wishful thinking about dreams just as one can about anything else. For my part I prefer to keep as close to the dream statement as possible, and to try to formulate it in accordance with its manifest meaning. If it proves impossible to relate this meaning to the conscious situation of the dreamer, then I frankly admit that I do not understand the dream, but I take good care not to juggle it into line with some preconceived theory.

4. CONCLUSION

947   I do not regard these statements as in any way a final proof
of my views, but simply as a conclusion from empirical premises
which I would like to submit to the consideration of my reader.
From the material before us I can derive no other hypothesis
that would adequately explain the facts (including the ESP
experiments). I am only too conscious that synchronicity is a
highly abstract and "irrepresentable" quantity. It ascribes to
the moving body a certain psychoid property which, like space,
time, and causality, forms a criterion of its behaviour. We must
completely give up the idea of the psyche's being somehow
connected with the brain, and remember instead the "meaningful" or "intelligent" behaviour of the lower organisms, which
are without a brain. Here we find ourselves much closer to the
formal factor which, as I have said, has nothing to do with
brain activity.

948   If that is so, then we must ask ourselves whether the relation
of soul and body can be considered from this angle, that is to
say whether the co-ordination of psychic and physical processes
in a living organism can be understood as a synchronistic phenomenon rather than as a causal relation. Both Geulincx and
Leibniz regarded the co-ordination of the psychic and the physical as an act of God, of some principle standing outside empirical nature. The assumption of a causal relation between psyche

and physis leads on the other hand to conclusions which it is difficult to square with experience: either there are physical processes which cause psychic happenings, or there is a pre-existent psyche which organizes matter. In the first case it is hard to see how chemical processes can ever produce psychic processes, and in the second case one wonders how an immaterial psyche could ever set matter in motion. It is not necessary to think of Leibniz's pre-established harmony or anything of that kind, which would have to be absolute and would manifest itself in a universal correspondence and sympathy, rather like the meaningful coincidence of time-points lying on the same degree of latitude in Schopenhauer. The synchronicity principle possesses properties that may help to clear up the body-soul problem. Above all it is the fact of causeless order, or rather, of meaningful orderedness, that may throw light on psychophysical parallelism. The "absolute knowledge" which is characteristic of synchronistic phenomena, a knowledge not mediated by the sense organs, supports the hypothesis of a self-subsistent meaning, or even expresses its existence. Such a form of existence can only be transcendental, since, as the knowledge of future or spatially distant events shows, it is contained in a psychically relative space and time, that is to say in an irrepresentable space-time continuum.

949   It may be worth our while to examine more closely, from this point of view, certain experiences which seem to indicate the existence of psychic processes in what are commonly held to be unconscious states. Here I am thinking chiefly of the remarkable observations made during deep syncopes resulting from acute brain injuries. Contrary to all expectations, a severe head injury is not always followed by a corresponding loss of consciousness. To the observer, the wounded man seems apathetic, "in a trance," and not conscious of anything. Subjectively, however, consciousness is by no means extinguished. Sensory communication with the outside world is in a large measure restricted, but is not always completely cut off, although the noise of battle, for instance, may suddenly give way to a "solemn" silence. In this state there is sometimes a very distinct and impressive sensation or hallucination of levitation, the wounded man seeming to rise into the air in the same position he was in at the moment he was wounded. If he was wounded standing up, he rises in a

standing position, if lying down, he rises in a lying position, if sitting, he rises in a sitting position. Occasionally his surroundings seem to rise with him—for instance the whole bunker in which he finds himself at the moment. The height of the levitation may be anything from eighteen inches to several yards. All feeling of weight is lost. In a few cases the wounded think they are making swimming movements with their arms. If there is any perception of their surroundings at all, it seems to be mostly imaginary, i.e., composed of memory images. During levitation the mood is predominantly euphoric. " 'Buoyant, solemn, heavenly, serene, relaxed, blissful, expectant, exciting' are the words used to describe it. . . . There are various kinds of 'ascension experiences.' " [1] Jantz and Beringer rightly point out that the wounded can be roused from their syncope by remarkably small stimuli, for instance if they are addressed by name or touched, whereas the most terrific bombardment has no effect.

950   Much the same thing can be observed in deep comas resulting from other causes. I would like to give an example from my own medical experience. A woman patient, whose reliability and truthfulness I have no reason to doubt, told me that her first birth was very difficult. After thirty hours of fruitless labour the doctor considered that a forceps delivery was indicated. This was carried out under light narcosis. She was badly torn and suffered great loss of blood. When the doctor, her mother, and her husband had gone, and everything was cleared up, the nurse wanted to eat, and the patient saw her turn round at the door and ask, "Do you want anything before I go to supper?" She tried to answer, but couldn't. She had the feeling that she was sinking through the bed into a bottomless void. She saw the nurse hurry to the bedside and seize her hand in order to take her pulse. From the way she moved her fingers to and fro the patient thought it must be almost imperceptible. Yet she herself felt quite all right, and was slightly amused at the nurse's alarm. She was not in the least frightened. That was the last she could remember for a long time. The next thing she was aware of was that, without feeling her body and its position, she was *looking down* from a point in the ceiling and could see everything going on in the room below her: she saw herself lying in the bed,

1 Hubert Jantz and Kurt Beringer, "Das Syndrom des Schwebeerlebnisses unmittelbar nach Kopfverletzungen," 202.

deadly pale, with closed eyes. Beside her stood the nurse. The doctor paced up and down the room excitedly, and it seemed to her that he had lost his head and didn't know what to do. Her relatives crowded to the door. Her mother and her husband came in and looked at her with frightened faces. She told herself it was too stupid of them to think she was going to die, for she would certainly come round again. All this time she knew that behind her was a glorious, park-like landscape shining in the brightest colours, and in particular an emerald green meadow with short grass, which sloped gently upwards beyond a wrought-iron gate leading into the park. It was spring, and little gay flowers such as she had never seen before were scattered about in the grass. The whole demesne sparkled in the sunlight, and all the colours were of an indescribable splendour. The sloping meadow was flanked on both sides by dark green trees. It gave her the impression of a clearing in the forest, never yet trodden by the foot of man. "I knew that this was the entrance to another world, and that if I turned round to gaze at the picture directly, I should feel tempted to go in at the gate, and thus step out of life." She did not actually *see* this landscape, as her back was turned to it, but she *knew* it was there. She felt there was nothing to stop her from entering in through the gate. She only knew that she would turn back to her body and would not die. That was why she found the agitation of the doctor and the distress of her relatives stupid and out of place.

951   The next thing that happened was that she awoke from her coma and saw the nurse bending over her in bed. She was told that she had been unconscious for about half an hour. The next day, some fifteen hours later, when she felt a little stronger, she made a remark to the nurse about the incompetent and "hysterical" behaviour of the doctor during her coma. The nurse energetically denied this criticism in the belief that the patient had been completely unconscious at the time and could therefore have known nothing of the scene. Only when she described in full detail what had happened during the coma was the nurse obliged to admit that the patient had perceived the events exactly as they happened in reality.

952   One might conjecture that this was simply a psychogenic twilight state in which a split-off part of consciousness still continued to function. The patient, however, had never been hys-

terical and had suffered a genuine heart collapse followed by syncope due to cerebral anaemia, as all the outward and evidently alarming symptoms indicated. She really was in a coma and ought to have had a complete psychic black-out and been altogether incapable of clear observation and sound judgment. The remarkable thing was that it was not an immediate perception of the situation through indirect or unconscious observation, but she saw the whole situation from *above,* as though "her eyes were in the ceiling," as she put it.

953   Indeed, it is not easy to explain how such unusually intense psychic processes can take place, and be remembered, in a state of severe collapse, and how the patient could observe actual events in concrete detail with closed eyes. One would expect such obvious cerebral anaemia to militate against or prevent the occurrence of highly complex psychic processes of that kind.

954   Sir Auckland Geddes presented a very similar case before the Royal Society of Medicine on February 26, 1927, though here the ESP went very much further. During a state of collapse the patient noted the splitting off of an integral consciousness from his bodily consciousness, the latter gradually resolving itself into its organ components. The other consciousness possessed verifiable ESP.[2]

955   These experiences seem to show that in swoon states, where by all human standards there is every guarantee that conscious activity and sense perception are suspended, consciousness, reproducible ideas, acts of judgment, and perceptions can still continue to exist. The accompanying feeling of levitation, alteration of the angle of vision, and extinction of hearing and of coenaesthetic perceptions indicate a shift in the localization of consciousness, a sort of separation from the body, or from the cerebral cortex or cerebrum which is conjectured to be the seat of conscious phenomena. If we are correct in this assumption, then we must ask ourselves whether there is some other nervous substrate in us, apart from the cerebrum, that can think and perceive, or whether the psychic processes that go on in us during loss of consciousness are synchronistic phenomena, i.e., events which have no causal connection with organic processes. This last possibility cannot be rejected out of hand in view of

[2] Cf. G. N. M. Tyrrell's report in *The Personality of Man,* pp. 197f. There is another case of this kind on pp. 199f.

93

the existence of ESP, i.e., of perceptions independent of space and time which cannot be explained as processes in the biological substrate. Where sense perceptions are impossible from the start, it can hardly be a question of anything but synchronicity. But where there are spatial and temporal conditions which would make perception and apperception possible in principle, and only the activity of consciousness, or the cortical function, is extinguished, and where, as in our example, a conscious phenomenon like perception and judgment nevertheless occurs, then the question of a nervous substrate might well be considered. It is well nigh axiomatic that conscious processes are tied to the cerebrum, and that the lower centres contain nothing but chains of reflexes which in themselves are unconscious. This is particularly true of the sympathetic system. Hence the insects, which have no cerebrospinal nervous system at all, but only a double chain of ganglia, are regarded as reflex automata.

956   This view has recently been challenged by the researches which von Frisch, of Graz, made into the life of bees. It turns out that bees not only tell their comrades, by means of a peculiar sort of dance, that they have found a feeding-place, but that they also indicate its direction and distance, thus enabling the beginners to fly to it directly.[3] This kind of message is no different in principle from information conveyed by a human being. In the latter case we would certainly regard such behaviour as a conscious and intentional act and can hardly imagine how anyone could prove in a court of law that it had taken place unconsciously. We could, at a pinch, admit on the basis of psychiatric experiences that objective information can in exceptional cases be communicated in a twilight state, but would expressly deny that communications of this kind are normally unconscious. Nevertheless it would be possible to suppose that in bees the process is unconscious. But that would not help to solve the problem, because we are still faced with the fact that the ganglionic system apparently achieves exactly the same result as our cerebral cortex. Nor is there any proof that bees are unconscious.

957   Thus we are driven to the conclusion that a nervous substrate like the sympathetic system, which is absolutely different

3 Karl von Frisch, *The Dancing Bees*, trans. by Dora Ilse, pp. 112ff.

from the cerebrospinal system in point of origin and function, can evidently produce thoughts and perceptions just as easily as the latter. What then are we to think of the sympathetic system in vertebrates? Can it also produce or transmit specifically psychic processes? Von Frisch's observations prove the existence of transcerebral thought and perception. One must bear this possibility in mind if we want to account for the existence of some form of consciousness during an unconscious coma. During a coma the sympathetic system is not paralysed and could therefore be considered as a possible carrier of psychic functions. If that is so, then one must ask whether the normal state of unconsciousness in sleep, and the potentially conscious dreams it contains, can be regarded in the same light—whether, in other words, dreams are produced not so much by the activity of the sleeping cortex, as by the unsleeping sympathetic system, and are therefore of a transcerebral nature.

958   Outside the realm of psychophysical parallelism, which we cannot at present pretend to understand, synchronicity is not a phenomenon whose regularity it is at all easy to demonstrate. One is as much impressed by the disharmony of things as one is surprised by their occasional harmony. In contrast to the idea of a pre-established harmony, the synchronistic factor merely stipulates the existence of an intellectually necessary principle which could be added as a fourth to the recognized triad of space, time, and causality. These factors are necessary but not absolute—most psychic contents are non-spatial, time and causality are psychically relative—and in the same way the synchronistic factor proves to be only conditionally valid. But unlike causality, which reigns despotically over the whole picture of the macrophysical world and whose universal rule is shattered only in certain lower orders of magnitude, synchronicity is a phenomenon that seems to be primarily connected with psychic conditions, that is to say with processes in the unconscious. Synchronistic phenomena are found to occur—experimentally— with some degree of regularity and frequency in the intuitive, "magical" procedures, where they are subjectively convincing but are extremely difficult to verify objectively and cannot be statistically evaluated (at least at present).

959   On the organic level it might be possible to regard biological morphogenesis in the light of the synchronistic factor. Professor

A. M. Dalcq (of Brussels) understands form, despite its tie with matter, as a "continuity that is supraordinate to the living organism." [4] Sir James Jeans reckons radioactive decay among the causeless events which, as we have seen, include synchronicity. He says: "Radioactive break-up appeared to be an effect without a cause, and suggested that the ultimate laws of nature were not even causal." [5] This highly paradoxical formula, coming from the pen of a physicist, is typical of the intellectual dilemma with which radioactive decay confronts us. It, or rather the phenomenon of "half-life," appears as an instance of acausal orderedness—a conception which also includes synchronicity and to which I shall revert below.

960 Synchronicity is not a philosophical view but an empirical concept which postulates an intellectually necessary principle. This cannot be called either materialism or metaphysics. No serious investigator would assert that the nature of what is observed to exist, and of that which observes, namely the psyche, are known and recognized quantities. If the latest conclusions of science are coming nearer and nearer to a unitary idea of being, characterized by space and time on the one hand and by causality and synchronicity on the other, that has nothing to do with materialism. Rather it seems to show that there is some possibility of getting rid of the incommensurability between the observed and the observer. The result, in that case, would be a unity of being which would have to be expressed in terms of a new conceptual language—a "neutral language," as W. Pauli once called it.

961 Space, time, and causality, the triad of classical physics, would then be supplemented by the synchronicity factor and become a tetrad, a *quaternio* which makes possible a whole judgment:

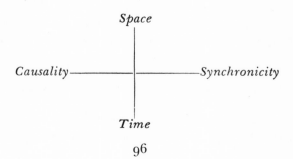

962   Here synchronicity is to the three other principles as the one-dimensionality of time [6] is to the three-dimensionality of space, or as the recalcitrant "Fourth" in the *Timaeus*, which, Plato says, can only be added "by force" to the other three.[7] Just as the introduction of time as the fourth dimension in modern physics postulates an irrepresentable space-time continuum, so the idea of synchronicity with its inherent quality of meaning produces a picture of the world so irrepresentable as to be completely baffling.[8] The advantage, however, of adding this concept is that it makes possible a view which includes the psychoid factor in our description and knowledge of nature—that is, an *a priori* meaning or "equivalence." The problem that runs like a red thread through the speculations of alchemists for fifteen hundred years thus repeats and solves itself, the so-called axiom of Maria the Jewess (or Copt): "Out of the Third comes the One as the Fourth." [9] This cryptic observation confirms what I said above, that in principle new points of view are not as a rule discovered in territory that is already known, but in out-of-the-way places that may even be avoided because of their bad name. The old dream of the alchemists, the transmutation of chemical elements, this much-derided idea, has become a reality in our own day, and its symbolism, which was no less an object of ridicule, has turned out to be a veritable gold-mine for the psychology of the unconscious. Their dilemma of three and four, which began with the story that serves as a setting for the *Timaeus* and extends all the way to the Cabiri scene in *Faust*, Part II, is recognized by a sixteenth-century alchemist, Gerhard Dorn, as the decision between the Christian Trinity and the *serpens quadricornutus*, the four-horned serpent who is the Devil. As though in anticipation of things to come he anathematizes the pagan quaternity which was ordinarily so beloved of the alche-

4 "La Morphogénèse dans la cadre de la biologie générale." Cf. above, the similar conclusion reached by the zoologist A. C. Hardy.

5 *Physics and Philosophy*, p. 127; cf. also p. 151.

6 I am not counting P. A. M. Dirac's multi-dimensionality of time.

7 Cf. my "Psychological Approach to the Dogma of the Trinity," pars. 186ff., 280, 290.

8 Sir James Jeans (*Physics and Philosophy*, p. 215) thinks it possible "that the springs of events in this substratum include our own mental activities, so that the future course of events may depend in part on these mental activities." The causalism of this argument does not seem to me altogether tenable.

9 "ἐκ τοῦ τρίτου τὸ ἓν τέταρτον." Cf. *Psychology and Alchemy*, par. 26.

mists, on the ground that it arose from the binarius (the number 2) and is thus something material, feminine, and devilish.[10] Dr. von Franz has demonstrated this emergence of trinitarian thinking in the *Parable* of Bernard of Treviso, in Khunrath's *Amphitheatrum,* in Michael Maier, and in the anonymous author of the *Aquarium sapientum.*[11] W. Pauli calls attention to the polemical writings of Kepler and of Robert Fludd, in which Fludd's correspondence theory was the loser and had to make room for Kepler's theory of three principles.[12] The decision in favour of the triad, which in certain respects ran counter to the alchemical tradition, was followed by a scientific epoch that knew nothing of correspondence and clung with passionate insistence to a triadic view of the world—a continuation of the trinitarian type of thinking—which described and explained everything in terms of space, time, and causality.

963 The revolution brought about by the discovery of radioactivity has considerably modified the classical views of physics. So great is the change of standpoint that we have to revise the classical schema I made use of above. As I was able, thanks to the friendly interest which Professor Pauli evinced in my work, to discuss these questions of principle with a professional physicist who could at the same time appreciate my psychological arguments, I am in a position to put forward a suggestion that takes modern physics into account. Pauli suggested replacing the opposition of space and time in the classical schema by (conservation of) energy and the space-time continuum. This suggestion led me to a closer definition of the other pair of opposites—causality and synchronicity—with a view to establishing some kind of connection between these two heterogeneous concepts. We finally agreed on the following *quaternio:*

Indestructible Energy

| *Constant Connection* *through Effect* *(Causality)* | *Inconstant Connection* *through Contingence,* *Equivalence, or "Meaning"* *(Synchronicity)* |

Space-Time Continuum

10 "De tenebris contra naturam," in *Theatrum chemicum,* I (1602), pp. 518ff.
11 Marie-Louise von Franz, "Die Parabel von der Fontina des Grafen von Tarvis."
12 See Pauli's contribution in *The Interpretation of Nature and the Psyche.*

964   This schema satisfies on the one hand the postulates of modern physics, and on the other hand those of psychology. The psychological point of view needs clarifying. A causalistic explanation of synchronicity seems out of the question for the reasons given above. It consists essentially of "chance" equivalences. Their *tertium comparationis* rests on the psychoid factors I call archetypes. These are *indefinite*, that is to say they can be known and determined only approximately. Although associated with causal processes, or "carried" by them, they continually go beyond their frame of reference, an infringement to which I would give the name "transgressivity," because the archetypes are not found exclusively in the psychic sphere, but can occur just as much in circumstances that are not psychic (equivalence of an outward physical process with a psychic one). Archetypal equivalences are *contingent* to causal determination, that is to say there exist between them and the causal processes no relations that conform to law. They seem, therefore, to represent a special instance of randomness or chance, or of that "random state" which "runs through time in a way that fully conforms to law," as Andreas Speiser says.[13] It is an initial state which is "not governed by mechanistic law" but is the precondition of law, the chance substrate on which law is based. If we consider synchronicity or the archetypes as the contingent, then the latter takes on the specific aspect of a modality that has the functional significance of a world-constituting factor. The archetype represents *psychic probability*, portraying ordinary instinctual events in the form of *types*. It is a special psychic instance of probability in general, which "is made up of the laws of chance and lays down rules for nature just as the laws of mechanics do."[14] We must agree with Speiser that although in the realm of pure intellect the contingent is "a formless substance," it reveals itself to psychic introspection—so far as inward perception can grasp it at all—as an image, or rather a type which underlies not only the psychic equivalences but, remarkably enough, the psychophysical equivalences too.

965   It is difficult to divest conceptual language of its causalistic colouring. Thus the word "underlying," despite its causalistic connotation, does not refer to anything causal, but simply to an

13 *Über die Freiheit*, 4f.   14 Ibid., p. 6.

existing quality, an irreducible contingency which is "Just-So." The meaningful coincidence or equivalence of a psychic and a physical state that have no causal relationship to one another means, in general terms, that it is a modality without a cause, an "acausal orderedness." The question now arises whether our definition of synchronicity with reference to the equivalence of psychic and physical processes is capable of expansion, or rather, requires expansion. This requirement seems to force itself on us when we consider the above, wider conception of synchronicity as an "acausal orderedness." Into this category come all "acts of creation," *a priori* factors such as the properties of natural numbers, the discontinuities of modern physics, etc. Consequently we would have to include constant and experimentally reproducible phenomena within the scope of our expanded concept, though this does not seem to accord with the nature of the phenomena included in synchronicity narrowly understood. The latter are mostly individual cases which cannot be repeated experimentally. This is not of course altogether true, as Rhine's experiments show and numerous other experiences with clairvoyant individuals. These facts prove that even in individual cases which have no common denominator and rank as "curiosities" there are certain regularities and therefore constant factors, from which we must conclude that our narrower conception of synchronicity is probably too narrow and really needs expanding. I incline in fact to the view that synchronicity in the narrow sense is only a particular instance of general acausal orderedness—that, namely, of the equivalence of psychic and physical processes where the observer is in the fortunate position of being able to recognize the *tertium comparationis*. But as soon as he perceives the archetypal background he is tempted to trace the mutual assimilation of independent psychic and physical processes back to a (causal) effect of the archetype, and thus to overlook the fact that they are merely contingent. This danger is avoided if one regards synchronicity as a special instance of general acausal orderedness. In this way we also avoid multiplying our principles of explanation illegitimately, for the archetype *is* the introspectively recognizable form of *a priori* psychic orderedness. If an external synchronistic process now associates itself with it, it falls into the same basic pattern—in other words, it too is "ordered." This form of orderedness differs from that of the properties of natural numbers or the discontinuities of physics in that the latter have existed from eternity and occur regularly, whereas the forms of psychic orderedness are *acts of creation in time*. That, incidentally, is precisely why I have stressed the element of time as being characteristic of these phenomena and called them *synchronistic*.

966   The modern discovery of discontinuity (e.g., the orderedness of energy quanta, of radium decay, etc.) has put an end to the sovereign rule of causality and thus to the triad of principles. The territory lost by the latter belonged earlier to the sphere of correspondence and sympathy, concepts which reached their greatest development in Leibniz's idea of pre-established harmony. Schopenhauer knew far too little about the empirical foundations of correspondence to realize how hopeless his causalistic attempt at explanation was. Today, thanks to the ESP experiments, we have a great deal of empirical material at our disposal. We can form some conception of its reliability when we learn from G. E. Hutchinson [15] that the ESP experiments conducted by S. G. Soal and K. M. Goldney have a probability of $1 : 10^{35}$, this being equivalent to the number of molecules in 250,000 tons of water. There are relatively few experiments in the field of the natural sciences whose results come anywhere near so high a degree of certainty. The exaggerated scepticism in regard to ESP is really without a shred of justification. The main reason for it is simply the ignorance which nowadays, unfortunately, seems to be the inevitable accompaniment of specialism and screens off the necessarily limited horizon of specialist studies from all higher and wider points of view in the most undesirable way. How often have we not found that the so-called "superstitions" contain a core of truth that is well worth knowing! It may well be that the originally magical significance of the word "wish," which is still preserved in "wishing-rod" (divining rod, or magic wand) and expresses not just wishing in the sense of desire but a magical action,[16] and

[15] S. G. Soal, "Science and Telepathy," p. 6.
[16] Jacob Grimm, *Teutonic Mythology*, trans. by J. S. Stallybrass, I, p. 137. Wish-objects are magic implements forged by dwarfs, such as Odin's spear Gungnir, Thor's hammer Mjollnir, and Freya's sword (II, p. 870). Wishing is "gotes kraft" (divine power). "Got hât an sie den wunsch geleit und der wünschelruoten hort"

the traditional belief in the efficacy of prayer, are both based on the experience of concomitant synchronistic phenomena.

967   Synchronicity is no more baffling or mysterious than the discontinuities of physics. It is only the ingrained belief in the sovereign power of causality that creates intellectual difficulties and makes it appear unthinkable that causeless events exist or could ever occur. But if they do, then we must regard them as *creative acts,* as the continuous creation [17] of a pattern that exists from all eternity, repeats itself sporadically, and is not derivable from any known antecedents. We must of course guard against thinking of every event whose cause is unknown as "causeless." This, as I have already stressed, is admissible only when a cause is not even thinkable. But thinkability is itself an idea that needs the most rigorous criticism. Had the atom [18] corresponded to the original philosophical conception of it, its fissionability would be unthinkable. But once it proves to be a measurable quantity, its non-fissionability becomes unthinkable. Meaningful coincidences are thinkable as pure chance. But the more they multiply and the greater and more exact the

---

(God has bestowed the wish on her and the treasure of [*or:* found by] the wishing-rod). "Beschoenen mit wunsches gewalte" (to make beautiful with the power of the wish) (IV, p. 1329). "Wish" = Sanskrit *manoratha,* literally, "car of the mind" or of the psyche, i.e., wish, desire, fancy. (A. A. Macdonell, *A Practical Sanskrit Dictionary,* s.v.)

[17] Continuous creation is to be thought of not only as a series of successive acts of creation, but also as the eternal presence of the *one* creative act, in the sense that God "was always the Father and always generated the Son" (Origen, *De principiis,* I, 2, 3), or that he is the "eternal Creator of minds" (Augustine, *Confessions,* XI, 31, trans. F. J. Sheed, p. 232). God is contained in his own creation, "nor does he stand in need of his own works, as if he had place in them where he might abide; but endures in his own eternity, where he abides and creates whatever pleases him, both in heaven and earth" (Augustine, on Ps. 113 : 14, in *Expositions on the Book of Psalms*). What happens successively in time is simultaneous in the mind of God: "An immutable order binds mutable things into a pattern, and in this order things which are not simultaneous in time exist simultaneously outside time" (Prosper of Aquitaine, *Sententiae ex Augustino delibatae,* XLI [Migne, *P.L.,* LI, col. 433]). "Temporal succession is without time in the eternal wisdom of God" (LVII [Migne, col. 455]). Before the Creation there was no time—time only began with created things: "Rather did time arise from the created than the created from time" (CCLXXX [Migne, col. 468]). "There was no time before time, but time was created together with the world" (Anon., *De triplici habitaculo,* VI [Migne, *P.L.,* XL, col. 995]).

[18] [From ἄτομος, 'indivisible, that cannot be cut.'—TRANS.]

correspondence is, the more their probability sinks and their unthinkability increases, until they can no longer be regarded as pure chance but, for lack of a causal explanation, have to be thought of as meaningful arrangements. As I have already said, however, their "inexplicability" is not due to the fact that the cause is unknown, but to the fact that a cause is not even thinkable in intellectual terms. This is necessarily the case when space and time lose their meaning or have become relative, for under those circumstances a causality which presupposes space and time for its continuance can no longer be said to exist and becomes altogether unthinkable.

968   For these reasons it seems to me necessary to introduce, alongside space, time, and causality, a category which not only enables us to understand synchronistic phenomena as a special class of natural events, but also takes the contingent partly as a universal factor existing from all eternity, and partly as the sum of countless individual acts of creation occurring in time.

ON SYNCHRONICITY [1]

969   It might seem appropriate to begin my exposition by defining the concept with which it deals. But I would rather approach the subject the other way and first give you a brief description of the facts which the concept of synchronicity is intended to cover. As its etymology shows, this term has something to do with time or, to be more accurate, with a kind of simultaneity. Instead of simultaneity we could also use the concept of a *meaningful coincidence* of two or more events, where something other than the probability of chance is involved. A statistical—that is, a probable—concurrence of events, such as the "duplication of cases" found in hospitals, falls within the category of chance. Groupings of this kind can consist of any number of terms and still remain within the framework of the probable and rationally possible. Thus, for instance, someone chances to notice the number on his street-car ticket. On arriving home he receives a telephone call during which the same number is men-

[1] [Originally given as a lecture, "Über Synchronizität," at the 1951 Eranos conference, Ascona, Switzerland, and published in the *Eranos-Jahrbuch 1951* (Zurich, 1952). The present translation was published in *Man and Time* (Papers from the Eranos Yearbooks, 3; New York and London, 1957); it is republished with minor revisions. The essay was, in the main, drawn from the preceding monograph. —Editors.]

tioned. In the evening he buys a theatre ticket that again has the same number. The three events form a chance grouping that, although not likely to occur often, nevertheless lies well within the framework of probability owing to the frequency of each of its terms. I would like to recount from my own experience the following chance grouping, made up of no fewer than six terms:

970   On April 1, 1949, I made a note in the morning of an inscription containing a figure that was half man and half fish. There was fish for lunch. Somebody mentioned the custom of making an "April fish" of someone. In the afternoon, a former patient of mine, whom I had not seen for months, showed me some impressive pictures of fish. In the evening, I was shown a piece of embroidery with sea monsters and fishes in it. The next morning, I saw a former patient, who was visiting me for the first time in ten years. She had dreamed of a large fish the night before. A few months later, when I was using this series for a larger work and had just finished writing it down, I walked over to a spot by the lake in front of the house, where I had already been several times that morning. This time a fish a foot long lay on the sea-wall. Since no one else was present, I have no idea how the fish could have got there.

971   When coincidences pile up in this way one cannot help being impressed by them—for the greater the number of terms in such a series, or the more unusual its character, the more improbable it becomes. For reasons that I have mentioned elsewhere and will not discuss now, I assume that this was a chance grouping. It must be admitted, though, that it is more improbable than a mere duplication.

972   In the above-mentioned case of the street-car ticket, I said that the observer "chanced" to notice the number and retain it in his memory, which ordinarily he would never have done. This formed the basis for the series of chance events, but I do not know what caused him to notice the number. It seems to me that in judging such a series a factor of uncertainty enters in at this point and requires attention. I have observed something similar in other cases, without, however, being able to draw any reliable conclusions. But it is sometimes difficult to avoid the impression that there is a sort of foreknowledge of the coming series of events. This feeling becomes irresistible when, as so frequently

happens, one thinks one is about to meet an old friend in the street, only to find to one's disappointment that it is a stranger. On turning the next corner one then runs into him in person. Cases of this kind occur in every conceivable form and by no means infrequently, but after the first momentary astonishment they are as a rule quickly forgotten.

973   Now, the more the foreseen details of an event pile up, the more definite is the impression of an existing foreknowledge, and the more improbable does chance become. I remember the story of a student friend whose father had promised him a trip to Spain if he passed his final examinations satisfactorily. My friend thereupon dreamed that he was walking through a Spanish city. The street led to a square, where there was a Gothic cathedral. He then turned right, around a corner, into another street. There he was met by an elegant carriage drawn by two cream-coloured horses. Then he woke up. He told us about the dream as we were sitting round a table drinking beer. Shortly afterward, having successfully passed his examinations, he went to Spain, and there, in one of the streets, he recognized the city of his dream. He found the square and the cathedral, which exactly corresponded to the dream-image. He wanted to go straight to the cathedral, but then remembered that in the dream he had turned right, at the corner, into another street. He was curious to find out whether his dream would be corroborated further. Hardly had he turned the corner when he saw in reality the carriage with the two cream-coloured horses.

974   The *sentiment du déjà-vu* is based, as I have found in a number of cases, on a foreknowledge in dreams, but we saw that this foreknowledge can also occur in the waking state. In such cases mere chance becomes highly improbable because the coincidence is known in advance. It thus loses its chance character not only psychologically and subjectively, but objectively too, since the accumulation of details that coincide immeasurably increases the improbability of chance as a determining factor. (For correct precognitions of death, Dariex and Flammarion have computed probabilities ranging from 1 in 4,000,000 to 1 in 8,000,-000.) [2] So in these cases it would be incongruous to speak of "chance" happenings. It is rather a question of meaningful coin-

---

[2] [For documentation, see supra, par. 830.—EDITORS.]

cidences. Usually they are explained by precognition—in other words, foreknowledge. People also talk of clairvoyance, telepathy, etc., without, however, being able to explain what these faculties consist of or what means of transmission they use in order to render events distant in space and time accessible to our perception. All these ideas are mere names; they are not scientific concepts which could be taken as statements of principle, for no one has yet succeeded in constructing a causal bridge between the elements making up a meaningful coincidence.

975   Great credit is due to J. B. Rhine for having established a reliable basis for work in the vast field of these phenomena by his experiments in extrasensory perception, or ESP. He used a pack of 25 cards divided into 5 groups of 5, each with its special sign (star, square, circle, cross, two wavy lines). The experiment was carried out as follows. In each series of experiments the pack is laid out 800 times, in such a way that the subject cannot see the cards. He is then asked to guess the cards as they are turned up. The probability of a correct answer is 1 in 5. The result, computed from very high figures, showed an average of 6.5 hits. The probability of a chance deviation of 1.5 amounts to only 1 in 250,000. Some individuals scored more than twice the probable number of hits. On one occasion all 25 cards were guessed correctly, which gives a probability of 1 in 298,023,223,-876,953,125. The spatial distance between experimenter and subject was increased from a few yards to about 4,000 miles, with no effect on the result.

976   A second type of experiment consisted in asking the subject to guess a series of cards that was still to be laid out in the near or more distant future. The time factor was increased from a few minutes to two weeks. The result of these experiments showed a probability of 1 in 400,000.

977   In a third type of experiment, the subject had to try to influence the fall of mechanically thrown dice by wishing for a certain number. The results of this so-called psychokinetic (PK) experiment were the more positive the more dice were used at a time.

978   The result of the spatial experiment proves with tolerable certainty that the psyche can, to some extent, eliminate the space factor. The time experiment proves that the time factor (at any

rate, in the dimension of the future) can become psychically relative. The experiment with dice proves that moving bodies, too, can be influenced psychically—a result that could have been predicted from the psychic relativity of space and time.

979   The energy postulate shows itself to be inapplicable to the Rhine experiments, and thus rules out all ideas about the transmission of force. Equally, the law of causality does not hold—a fact that I pointed out thirty years ago. For we cannot conceive how a future event could bring about an event in the present. Since for the time being there is no possibility whatever of a causal explanation, we must assume provisionally that improbable accidents of an acausal nature—that is, meaningful coincidences—have entered the picture.

980   In considering these remarkable results we must take into account a fact discovered by Rhine, namely that in each series of experiments the first attempts yielded a better result than the later ones. The falling off in the number of hits scored was connected with the mood of the subject. An initial mood of faith and optimism makes for good results. Scepticism and resistance have the opposite effect, that is, they create an unfavourable disposition. As the energic, and hence also the causal, approach to these experiments has shown itself to be inapplicable, it follows that the affective factor has the significance simply of a *condition* which makes it possible for the phenomenon to occur, though it need not. According to Rhine's results, we may nevertheless expect 6.5 hits instead of only 5. But it cannot be predicted in advance when the hit will come. Could we do so, we would be dealing with a law, and this would contradict the entire nature of the phenomenon. It has, as said, the improbable character of a "lucky hit" or accident that occurs with a more than merely probable frequency and is as a rule dependent on a certain state of affectivity.

981   This observation has been thoroughly confirmed, and it suggests that the psychic factor which modifies or even eliminates the principles underlying the physicist's picture of the world is connected with the affective state of the subject. Although the phenomenology of the ESP and PK experiments could be considerably enriched by further experiments of the kind described above, deeper investigation of its bases will have to concern itself with the nature of the affectivity involved. I have there-

fore directed my attention to certain observations and experiences which, I can fairly say, have forced themselves upon me during the course of my long medical practice. They have to do with spontaneous, meaningful coincidences of so high a degree of improbability as to appear flatly unbelievable. I shall therefore describe to you only one case of this kind, simply to give an example characteristic of a whole category of phenomena. It makes no difference whether you refuse to believe this particular case or whether you dispose of it with an *ad hoc* explanation. I could tell you a great many such stories, which are in principle no more surprising or incredible than the irrefutable results arrived at by Rhine, and you would soon see that almost every case calls for its own explanation. But the causal explanation, the only possible one from the standpoint of natural science, breaks down owing to the psychic relativization of space and time, which together form the indispensable premises for the cause-and-effect relationship.

982   My example concerns a young woman patient who, in spite of efforts made on both sides, proved to be psychologically inaccessible. The difficulty lay in the fact that she always knew better about everything. Her excellent education had provided her with a weapon ideally suited to this purpose, namely a highly polished Cartesian rationalism with an impeccably "geometrical" [3] idea of reality. After several fruitless attempts to sweeten her rationalism with a somewhat more human understanding, I had to confine myself to the hope that something unexpected and irrational would turn up, something that would burst the intellectual retort into which she had sealed herself. Well, I was sitting opposite her one day, with my back to the window, listening to her flow of rhetoric. She had had an impressive dream the night before, in which someone had given her a golden scarab—a costly piece of jewellery. While she was still telling me this dream, I heard something behind me gently tapping on the window. I turned round and saw that it was a fairly large flying insect that was knocking against the window-pane from outside in the obvious effort to get into the dark room. This seemed to me very strange. I opened the window immediately and caught the insect in the air as it flew in. It was a scarabaeid beetle, or

3 [Descartes demonstrated his propositions by the "Geometrical Method."— EDITORS.]

common rose-chafer (*Cetonia aurata*), whose gold-green colour most nearly resembles that of a golden scarab. I handed the beetle to my patient with the words, "Here is your scarab." This experience punctured the desired hole in her rationalism and broke the ice of her intellectual resistance. The treatment could now be continued with satisfactory results.

983   This story is meant only as a paradigm of the innumerable cases of meaningful coincidence that have been observed not only by me but by many others, and recorded in large collections. They include everything that goes by the name of clairvoyance, telepathy, etc., from Swedenborg's well-attested vision of the great fire in Stockholm to the recent report by Air Marshal Sir Victor Goddard about the dream of an unknown officer, which predicted the subsequent accident to Goddard's plane.[4]

984   All the phenomena I have mentioned can be grouped under three categories:

1. The coincidence of a psychic state in the observer with a simultaneous, objective, external event that corresponds to the psychic state or content (e.g., the scarab), where there is no evidence of a causal connection between the psychic state and the external event, and where, considering the psychic relativity of space and time, such a connection is not even conceivable.

2. The coincidence of a psychic state with a corresponding (more or less simultaneous) external event taking place outside the observer's field of perception, i.e., at a distance, and only verifiable afterward (e.g., the Stockholm fire).

3. The coincidence of a psychic state with a corresponding, not yet existent future event that is distant in time and can likewise only be verified afterward.

985   In groups 2 and 3 the coinciding events are not yet present in the observer's field of perception, but have been anticipated in time in so far as they can only be verified afterward. For this reason I call such events *synchronistic,* which is not to be confused with *synchronous.*

986   Our survey of this wide field of experience would be incomplete if we failed to take into account the so-called mantic methods. Manticism lays claim, if not actually to producing synchronistic events, then at least to making them serve its ends.

4 [This case was the subject of an English film, *The Night My Number Came Up.*—EDITORS.]

An example of this is the oracle method of the *I Ching*, which Dr. Hellmut Wilhelm has described in detail.[5] The *I Ching* presupposes that there is a synchronistic correspondence between the psychic state of the questioner and the answering hexagram. The hexagram is formed either by the random division of the 49 yarrow stalks or by the equally random throw of three coins. The result of this method is, incontestably, very interesting, but so far as I can see it does not provide any tool for an objective determination of the facts, that is to say a statistical evaluation, since the psychic state in question is much too indefinite and indefinable. The same holds true of the geomantic experiment, which is based on similar principles.

987   We are in a somewhat more favourable situation when we turn to the astrological method, as it presupposes a meaningful coincidence of planetary aspects and positions with the character or the existing psychic state of the questioner. In the light of the most recent astrophysical research, astrological correspondence is probably not a matter of synchronicity but, very largely, of a causal relationship. As Professor Max Knoll has demonstrated,[6] the solar proton radiation is influenced to such a degree by planetary conjunctions, oppositions, and quartile aspects that the appearance of magnetic storms can be predicted with a fair amount of probability. Relationships can be established between the curve of the earth's magnetic disturbances and the mortality rate that confirm the unfavourable influence of conjunctions, oppositions, and quartile aspects and the favourable influence of trine and sextile aspects. So it is probably a question here of a causal relationship, i.e., of a natural law that excludes synchronicity or restricts it. At the same time, the zodiacal qualification of the houses, which plays a large part in the horoscope, creates a complication in that the astrological zodiac, although agreeing with the calendar, does not coincide with the actual constellations themselves. These have shifted their positions by almost a whole platonic month as a result of the precession of the equinoxes since the time when the springpoint was in zero Aries, about the beginning of our era. Therefore, anyone born in Aries today (according to the calendar) is

5 ["The Concept of Time in the Book of Changes," originally a lecture at the 1951 Eranos conference.—EDITORS.]
6 ["Transformations of Science in Our Age," ibid.]

actually born in Pisces. It is simply that his birth took place at a time which, for approximately 2,000 years, has been called "Aries." Astrology presupposes that this time has a determining quality. It is possible that this quality, like the disturbances in the earth's magnetic field, is connected with the seasonal fluctuations to which solar proton radiation is subject. It is therefore not beyond the realm of possibility that the zodiacal positions may also represent a causal factor.

988 Although the psychological interpretation of horoscopes is still a very uncertain matter, there is nevertheless some prospect today of a causal explanation in conformity with natural law. Consequently, we are no longer justified in describing astrology as a mantic method. Astrology is in the process of becoming a science. But as there are still large areas of uncertainty, I decided some time ago to make a test and find out how far an accepted astrological tradition would stand up to statistical investigation. For this purpose it was necessary to select a definite and indisputable fact. My choice fell on marriage. Since antiquity, the traditional belief in regard to marriage has been that there is a conjunction of sun and moon in the horoscope of the marriage partners, that is, ☉ (sun) with an orbit of 8 degrees in the case of one partner, in ☌ (conjunction) with ☾ (moon) in the case of the other. A second, equally old, tradition takes ☾ ☌ ☾ as another marriage characteristic. Of like importance are the conjunctions of the ascendent (*Asc.*) with the large luminaries.

989 Together with my co-worker, Mrs. Liliane Frey-Rohn, I first proceeded to collect 180 marriages, that is to say, 360 horoscopes,[7] and compared the 50 most important aspects that might possibly be characteristic of marriage, namely the conjunctions and oppositions of ☉ ☾ ♂ (Mars) ♀ (Venus) *Asc.* and *Desc.* This resulted in a maximum of 10 per cent for ☉ ☌ ☾. As Professor Markus Fierz, of Basel, who kindly went to the trouble of computing the probability of my result, informed me, my figure has a probability of 1 : 10,000. The opinion of several mathematical physicists whom I consulted about the significance of this figure is divided: some find it considerable, others find it of question-

7 This material stemmed from different sources. They were simply horoscopes of married people. There was no selection of any kind. We took at random all the marriage horoscopes we could lay hands on.

able value. Our figure is inconclusive inasmuch as a total of 360 horoscopes is far too small from a statistical point of view.

990 While the aspects of these 180 marriages were being worked out statistically, our collection was enlarged, and when we had collected 220 more marriages, this batch was subjected to separate investigation. As on the first occasion, the material was evaluated just as it came in. It was not selected from any special point of view and was drawn from the most varied sources. Evaluation of this second batch yielded a maximum figure of 10.9 per cent for ☾ ☌ ☾. The probability of this figure is also about 1 : 10,000.

991 Finally, 83 more marriages arrived, and these in turn were investigated separately. The result was a maximum figure of 9.6 per cent for ☾ ☌ *Asc.* The probability of this figure is approximately 1 : 3,000.[8]

992 One is immediately struck by the fact that the conjunctions are all *moon conjunctions,* which is in accord with astrological expectations. But the strange thing is that what has turned up here are the three basic positions of the horoscope, ☉ ☾ and *Asc.* The probability of a concurrence of ☉ ☌ ☾ and ☾ ☌ ☾ amounts to 1 : 100,000,000. The concurrence of the three moon conjunctions with ☉ ☾ *Asc.* has a probability of $1 : 3 \times 10^{11}$; in other words, the improbability of its being due to mere chance is so enormous that we are forced to take into account the existence of some factor responsible for it. The three batches were so small that little or no theoretical significance can be attached to the individual probabilities of 1 : 10,000 and 1 : 3,000. Their concurrence, however, is so improbable that one cannot help assuming the existence of an impelling factor that produced this result.

993 The possibility of there being a scientifically valid connection between astrological data and proton radiation cannot be held responsible for this, since the individual probabilities of 1 : 10,000 and 1 : 3,000 are too great for us to be able, with any degree of certainty, to view our result as other than mere chance. Besides, the maxima cancel each other out as soon as one divides up the marriages into a larger number of batches. It would require hundreds of thousands of marriage horoscopes to establish

8 [These and the following figures were later revised by Professor Fierz and considerably reduced. See supra, pars. 901ff.—EDITORS.]

the statistical regularity of occurrences like the sun, moon, and ascendent conjunctions, and even then the result would be questionable. That anything so improbable as the turning up of the three classical moon conjunctions should occur at all, however, can only be explained either as the result of an intentional or unintentional fraud, or else as precisely such a meaningful coincidence, that is, as synchronicity.

994   Although I was obliged to express doubt, earlier, about the mantic character of astrology, I am now forced as a result of my astrological experiment to recognize it again. The chance arrangement of the marriage horoscopes, which were simply piled on top of one another as they came in from the most diverse sources, and the equally fortuitous way they were divided into three unequal batches, suited the sanguine expectations of the research workers and produced an over-all picture that could scarcely have been improved upon from the standpoint of the astrological hypothesis. The success of the experiment is entirely in accord with Rhine's ESP results, which were also favorably affected by expectation, hope, and faith. However, there was no definite expectation of any one result. Our selection of 50 aspects is proof of this. After we got the result of the first batch, a slight expectation did exist that the ☉ ☌ ☽ would be confirmed. But we were disappointed. The second time, we made up a larger batch from the newly added horoscopes in order to increase the element of certainty. But the result was ☽ ☌ ☽. With the third batch, there was only a faint expectation that ☽ ☌ ☽ would be confirmed, but again this was not the case.

995   What happened in this case was admittedly a curiosity, apparently a unique instance of meaningful coincidence. If one is impressed by such things, one could call it a minor miracle. Today, however, we are obliged to view the miraculous in a somewhat different light. The Rhine experiments have demonstrated that space and time, and hence causality, are factors that can be eliminated, with the result that acausal phenomena, otherwise called miracles, appear possible. All natural phenomena of this kind are unique and exceedingly curious combinations of chance, held together by the common meaning of their parts to form an unmistakable whole. Although meaningful coincidences are infinitely varied in their phenomenology, as acausal events they nevertheless form an element that is part

of the scientific picture of the world. Causality is the way we explain the link between two successive events. Synchronicity designates the parallelism of time and meaning between psychic and psychophysical events, which scientific knowledge so far has been unable to reduce to a common principle. The term explains nothing, it simply formulates the occurrence of meaningful coincidences which, in themselves, are chance happenings, but are so improbable that we must assume them to be based on some kind of principle, or on some property of the empirical world. No reciprocal causal connection can be shown to obtain between parallel events, which is just what gives them their chance character. The only recognizable and demonstrable link between them is a common meaning, or equivalence. The old theory of correspondence was based on the experience of such connections—a theory that reached its culminating point and also its provisional end in Leibniz' idea of pre-established harmony, and was then replaced by causality. Synchronicity is a modern differentiation of the obsolete concept of correspondence, sympathy, and harmony. It is based not on philosophical assumptions but on empirical experience and experimentation.

996   Synchronistic phenomena prove the simultaneous occurrence of meaningful equivalences in heterogeneous, causally unrelated processes; in other words, they prove that a content perceived by an observer can, at the same time, be represented by an outside event, without any causal connection. From this it follows either that the psyche cannot be localized in space, or that space is relative to the psyche. The same applies to the temporal determination of the psyche and the psychic relativity of time. I do not need to emphasize that the verification of these findings must have far-reaching consequences.

997   In the short space of a lecture I cannot, unfortunately, do more than give a very cursory sketch of the vast problem of synchronicity. For those of you who would care to go into this question more deeply, I would mention that a more extensive work of mine is soon to appear under the title "Synchronicity: An Acausal Connecting Principle." It will be published together with a work by Professor W. Pauli in a book called *The Interpretation of Nature and the Psyche*.[9]

9 [See the foregoing.—EDITORS.]

BIBLIOGRAPHY

BIBLIOGRAPHY

ABEGG, LILY. *The Mind of East Asia*. London and New York, 1952.

AGRIPPA VON NETTESHEIM, HEINRICH (HENRICUS) CORNELIUS. *De occulta philosophia libri tres*. Cologne, 1533. For translation, see: *Three Books of Occult Philosophy*. Translated by "J. F." London, 1651. Republished (Book I only) as: *The Occult Philosophy or Magic*. Edited by Willis F. Whitehead. Chicago, 1898.

ALBERTUS MAGNUS. *De mirabilibus mundi*. Incunabulum, undated, in the Zentralbibliothek, Zurich. (There is an edn. printed at Cologne, 1485.)

ANONYMOUS. *De triplici habitaculo*. See MIGNE, *P.L.*, vol. 40, cols. 991–98.

AUGUSTINE, SAINT. *Confessions*. Translated by Francis Joseph Sheed. London and New York, 1951.

———. *Expositions on the Book of Psalms*. Translated by J. Tweed, T. Scratton, and others. (Library of the Fathers of the Holy Catholic Church.) Oxford, 1847–57. 6 vols.

BÖHME, JAKOB. *De signatura rerum*. Amsterdam, 1635. For translation, see: *The Signature of All Things*. Translated by John Ellistone, edited by Clifford Bax. (Everyman's Library.) London and New York, 1912.

BROWN, G. SPENCER. "De la recherche psychique considérée comme un test de la théorie des probabilités," *Revue métapsychique* (Paris), no. 29–30 (May–Aug. 1954), 87–96.

CARDAN, JEROME (Hieronymus Cardanus). *Commentaria in Ptolemaeum De astrorum judiciis*. In: *Opera omnia*. Lyons, 1663. 10 vols. (V, 93–368.)

DAHNS, FRITZ. "Das Schwärmen des Palolo," *Der Naturforscher* (Berlin), VIII (1932), 379–82.

DALCQ, A. M. "La Morphogenèse dans la cadre de la biologie générale," *Verhandlungen der Schweizerischen naturforschenden Gesellschaft* (129th Annual Meeting at Lausanne; pub. at Aarau), 1949, 37–72.

DIETERICH, ALBRECHT. *Eine Mithrasliturgie*. Leipzig, 1903; 2nd edn., 1910.

DRIESCH, HANS. *Philosophie des Organischen.* Leipzig, 1909. 2 vols. 2nd edn., Leipzig, 1921. 1 vol. For translation, see: *The Science and Philosophy of the Organism.* 2nd edn., London, 1929.

——. *Die "Seele" als elementarer Naturfaktor.* Leipzig, 1903.

DUNNE, JOHN WILLIAM. *An Experiment with Time.* London, 1927; 2nd edn., New York, 1938.

ECKERMANN, J. P. *Conversations with Goethe.* Translated by R. O. Moon. London [1951].

FIERZ, MARKUS. "Zur physikalischen Erkenntnis," *Eranos-Jahrbuch 1948* (Zurich, 1949), 433-460.

FLAMBART, PAUL. *Preuves et bases de l'astrologie scientifique.* Paris, 1921.

FLAMMARION, CAMILLE. *The Unknown.* London and New York, 1900.

FLUDD, ROBERT. [*De arte geomantica.*] "Animae intellectualis scientia seu De geomantia." In: *Fasciculus geomanticus, in quo varia variorum opera geomantica.* Verona, 1687.

FRANZ, MARIE-LOUISE VON. "Die Parabel von der Fontina des Grafen von Tarvis." Unpublished.

——. "Die Passio Perpetuae." In: C. G. JUNG. *Aion.* Zurich, 1951.

FRISCH, KARL VON. *The Dancing Bees.* Translated by Dora Ilse. New York and London, 1954.

GEULINCX, ARNOLD. *Opera philosophica.* Edited by J. P. N. Land. The Hague, 1891–99. 3 vols. (Vol. II: *Metaphysica vera.*)

GRIMM, JACOB. *Teutonic Mythology.* Translated by J. S. Stallybrass. London, 1883–88. 4 vols.

GURNEY, EDMUND; MYERS, FREDERIC W. H.; and PODMORE, FRANK. *Phantasms of the Living.* London, 1886. 2 vols.

HARDY, A. C. See: "The Scientific Evidence for Extra-Sensory Perception," in Report of the British Association Meeting at Newcastle, 31 Aug.–7 Sept., 1949, *Discovery* (London), X (1949), 348.

HIPPOCRATES (ascribed to). *De alimento.* In: *Hippocrates on Diet and Hygiene.* Translated by John Precope. London, 1952.

I Ching. The German translation by Richard Wilhelm, rendered into English by Cary F. Baynes. New York (Bollingen Series XIX), 1950; London, 1951. 2 vols.; 2nd edn., 1 vol., 1961; 3rd edn., revised, Princeton and London, 1967.

ISIDORE OF SEVILLE, SAINT. *Liber etymologiarum.* See MIGNE, *P.L.*, vol. 82, cols. 73–728.

JAFFÉ, ANIELA. "Bilder und Symbole aus E. T. A. Hoffmanns Märchen 'Der Goldene Topf'." In: C. G. JUNG. *Gestaltungen des Unbewussten*. Zurich, 1950.

JANTZ, HUBERT, and BERINGER, KURT. "Das Syndrom des Schwebeerlebnisses unmittelbar nach Kopfverletzungen," *Der Nervenarzt* (Berlin), XVII (1944), 197–206.

JEANS, JAMES. *Physics and Philosophy*. Cambridge, 1942.

JORDAN, PASCUAL. "Positivistische Bemerkungen über die parapsychischen Erscheinungen," *Zentralblatt für Psychotherapie* (Leipzig), IX (1936), 3–17.

———. *Verdrängung und Komplementarität*. Hamburg, 1947.

JUNG, CARL GUSTAV. *Collected Papers on Analytical Psychology*. Edited by Constance E. Long, translated by various hands. London and New York, 1916; 2nd edn., 1917.

———. Commentary on *The Secret of the Golden Flower*. In: *Alchemical Studies*, q.v.; see also WILHELM, RICHARD.

———. "Concerning Mandala Symbolism." In: *The Archetypes and the Collective Unconscious*, Collected Works, 9, i.

———. "On the Psychology of Eastern Meditation." In: *Psychology and Religion: West and East*. Collected Works, 11.

———. "Paracelsus as a Spiritual Phenomenon." In: *Alchemical Studies*. Collected Works, 13. (Alternate source: "Paracelsus als geistige Erscheinung," *Paracelsica*, Zurich, 1942.)

———. "A Psychological Approach to the Dogma of the Trinity." In: *Psychology and Religion: West and East*. Collected Works, 11.

———. *Psychology and Alchemy*. Collected Works, 12.

———. "The Spirit Mercurius." In: *Alchemical Studies*. Collected Works, 13.

———. "Studies in Word Association." Part I of *Experimental Researches*. Collected Works, 2.

———. "A Study in the Process of Individuation." In: *The Archetypes and the Collective Unconscious*. Collected Works, 9, i.

KAMMERER, PAUL. *Das Gesetz der Serie*. Stuttgart and Berlin, 1919.

KANT, IMMANUEL. *Dreams of a Spirit-Seer, Illustrated by Dreams of Metaphysics*. Translated by Emanuel F. Goerwitz. London, 1900.

KEPLER, JOHANNES. *Gesammelte Werke*. Edited by Max Caspar and others. Munich, 1937ff. (Vol. IV: *Kleinere Schriften (1602–1611)*. Edited by Max Caspar and Franz Hammer. 1941.)

[KEPLER, JOHANNES.] *Joannis Kepleri astronomi Opera omnia.* Edited by C. Frisch. Frankfurt and Erlangen, 1858–71. 8 vols.

KLOECKLER, HERBERT VON. *Astrologie als Erfahrungswissenschaft.* Leipzig, 1927.

KNOLL, MAX. "Transformations of Science in Our Age." In *Man and Time,* q.v.

KRAFFT, K. E.; BUDAI, E.; and FERRIÈRE, A. *Le Premier Traité d'astro-biologie.* Paris, 1939.

KRÄMER, AUGUSTIN FRIEDRICH. *Über den Bau der Korallenriffe.* Kiel and Leipzig, 1897.

KRONECKER, LEOPOLD. *Werke.* Leipzig, 1895–1930. 5 vols.

LEIBNIZ, GOTTFRIED WILHELM. *Kleinere philosophische Schriften.* Edited by R. Habs. Leipzig, 1883. 3 vols.

———. *Philosophical Writings.* Selected and translated by Mary Morris. (Everyman's Library.) London and New York, 1934. (*Monadology,* pp. 3–20; *Principles of Nature and of Grace, founded on Reason,* pp. 21–31.)

[———.] *The Philosophical Works of Leibniz; a Selection.* Translated by G. M. Duncan. New Haven, 1890.

———. *Theodicy.* Translated by E. M. Huggard. Edited by Austin Farrer. London, 1951 [1952].

MEIER, CARL ALFRED. *Zeitgemässe Probleme der Traumforschung.* (Eidgenössische Technische Hochschule: Kultur- und Staatswissenschaftliche Schriften, 75.) Zurich, 1950.

MIGNE, JACQUES PAUL (ed.). *Patrologiae cursus completus.*
[*P.L.*] Latin series. Paris, 1844–64. 221 vols.
[*P.G.*] Greek series. Paris, 1857–66. 166 vols.
[These works are cited as "MIGNE, *P.L.*" and "MIGNE, *P.G.*" respectively. References are to columns, not to pages.]

ORIGEN. *De principiis.* See MIGNE, *P.G.,* vol. 11, cols. 115–414. For translation, see: *On First Principles.* Translated by G. W. Butterworth. London, 1936.

PARACELSUS (Theophrastus Bombastes of Hohenheim). *Das Buch Paragranum.* Edited by Franz Strunz. Leipzig, 1903.

———. *Sämtliche Werke.* Edited by Karl Sudhoff and Wilhelm Matthiessen. Munich and Berlin, 1922–35. 15 vols.

PAULI, W. "The Influence of Archetypal Ideas on the Scientific Theories of Kepler." Translated by Priscilla Silz. In: *The Interpretation of Nature and the Psyche.* New York (Bollingen Series LI) and London, 1955.

PHILO JUDAEUS. *De opificio mundi*. In: [*Works*]. Translated by F. H. Colson and G. H. Whitaker. (Loeb Classical Library.) New York and London, 1929– . 12 vols. [I, 2–137.]

PICO DELLA MIRANDOLA. *Opera omnia*. Basel, 1557.

PLOTINUS. *The Enneads*. Translated by Stephen Mackenna. 2nd edn., revised by B. S. Page. London, 1956.

PRATT, J. G.; RHINE, J. B.; STUART, C. E.; SMITH, B. M.; and GREENWOOD, J. A. *Extra-Sensory Perception after Sixty Years*. New York, 1940.

PROSPER OF AQUITAINE. *Sententiae ex Augustino delibatae*. See MIGNE, *P.L.*, vol. 51, cols. 427–496.

PTOLEMAEUS (Ptolemy). See CARDAN, JEROME.

REID, THOMAS. *Essays on the Active Powers of Man*. Edinburgh, 1788.

RHINE, J. B. *Extra-Sensory Perception*. Boston, 1934.

———. "An Introduction to the Work of Extra-Sensory Perception," *Transactions of the New York Academy of Sciences* (New York), Ser. II, XII (1950), 164-68.

———. *New Frontiers of the Mind*. New York and London, 1937.

———. *The Reach of the Mind*. London, 1948. Reprinted Harmondsworth (Penguin Books), 1954.

——— and HUMPHREY, BETTY M. "A Transoceanic ESP Experiment," *Journal of Parapsychology* (Durham, North Carolina), VI (1942), 52–74.

RICHET, CHARLES. "Relations de diverses expériences sur transmission mentale, la lucidité, et autres phénomènes non explicable par les données scientifiques actuelles," *Proceedings of the Society for Psychical Research* (London), V (1888), 18–168.

SCHILLER, FRIEDRICH. "The Cranes of Ibycus." In: *The Poems*. Translated by E. P. Arnold-Forster. London, 1901. (Pp. 158-63.)

SCHMIEDLER, G. R. "Personality Correlates of ESP as Shown by Rorschach Studies," *Journal of Parapsychology* (Durham, North Carolina), XIII (1949), 23–31.

SCHOLZ, WILHELM VON. *Der Zufall: eine Vorform des Schicksals*. Stuttgart, 1924.

SCHOPENHAUER, ARTHUR. *Parerga und Paralipomena*. Edited by R. von Koeber. Berlin, 1891. 2 vols.

SOAL, S. G. "Science and Telepathy," *Enquiry* (London), I:2 (1948), 5-7.

SOAL, S. G. and BATEMAN, F. *Modern Experiments in Telepathy.* London, 1954.

SPEISER, ANDREAS. *Über die Freiheit.* (Basler Universitätsreden, 28.) Basel, 1950.

THORNDIKE, LYNN. *A History of Magic and Experimental Science.* New York, 1929–41. 6 vols.

TYRRELL, G. N. M. *The Personality of Man.* London, 1947.

VIRGIL. *[Works].* Translated by H. Rushton Fairclough. (Loeb Classical Library.) London and New York, 1929. 2 vols.

WALEY, ARTHUR (trans.). *The Way and Its Power.* London, 1934.

[WEI PO-YANG.] "An Ancient Chinese Treatise on Alchemy entitled Ts'an T'ung Ch'i" (translated by Lu-chiang Wu), *Isis* (Bruges), XVIII (1932), 210–89.

WEYL, HERMANN. "Wissenschaft als symbolische Konstruktion des Menschen," *Eranos-Jahrbuch 1948* (Zurich, 1949), 375–439.

WILHELM, HELLMUT. "The Concept of Time in the Book of Changes." In *Man and Time,* q.v.

WILHELM, RICHARD. *Chinesische Lebensweisheit.* Darmstadt, 1922.

——— (trans.). *The Secret of the Golden Flower.* With a commentary and a memorial by C. G. Jung. London and New York, 1931; 2nd edn., revised, 1962. Jung's commentary in his *Alchemical Studies,* q.v.

———. *Das wahre Buch vom südlichen Blütenland.* Jena, 1912.

———. See also *I Ching.*

ZELLER, EDUARD. *Die Philosophie der Griechen in ihrer geschichtlichen Entwicklung dargestellt.* Tübingen, 1856. 3 vols.

INDEX

INDEX

fish: April, 10, 105; in example of
  synchronicity, 10, 11n, 105;
  symbol, 3
Flambart, Paul, 38
Flammarion, Camille, 14f, 106
flowers, 80
Fludd, Robert, 37n, 98
force: transmission of, 108
foreknowledge, 77, 105, 106
form, 96
Fortgibu, M. de, 15
Franz, Marie-Louise von, 79n, 84n,
  98
Freya, 101n
Frey-Rohn, Liliane, 58, 112
Frisch, Karl von, 94, 95

G

Galileo, 33
ganglia: in insects, 94
Garrett, Eileen J., 18
Gauss, Karl Friedrich, 86
Geddes, Sir Auckland, 93
geomantic experiment, 111
geometria, 80
geometry, 81
"getting stuck," 24
Geulincx, Arnold, 33, 82n, 89
God: creator/ and creation, 102n;
  always Father, 102n; knowledge
  and will in, 84; world as visible/
  world-system as, 75
Goddard, Air Marshal Sir Victor,
  110
gods: all things full of, 77
Goethe, Johann Wolfgang von, 33,
  39n, 97
Goldney, K. M., 101
Granet, Marcel, 73
graphology, 38
Grimm, Jacob, 101n
Gungnir, 101n
Gurney, E., 14n, 34

H

Hades, Babylonian, 23
half-life, 96
hallucination(s), 90
hammer, Thor's, 101n
Hardy, A. C., 78, 97n
harmony: pre-established, 12, 14,
  82ff, 90, 95, 101, 115
head(s): carved in rock, dream of,
  88; in relief, dream of, 87
hearing, extinction of, 93
heaven(s): man and, 74, 79, 80
Heraclitus, 69
hexagrams, see *I Ching*
hieros gamos, 59
Hippocrates, 73f, 76
Homer, 22n
horoscope, 38, 39n, 43ff, 112; *see
  also* astrology
house(s): astrological, 37, 39n, 111
Hutchinson, G. E., 101

I

Ibycus, 26n
I Ching, 34ff, 58, 110
image(s): perceiving consisting of,
  78
imitation, 9
immediacy, of events, 31
impossibility, 24, 25
inertia, 9
injuries, brain, 90
insects, 94
instinct(s), and affectivity, 24
interest, and telepathic experiments, 15
interpretations, unconscious, 15
intuition(s), 35
ionosphere, 44
Isidore of Seville, 37n

J

Jacobi, K. G. J., 86
Jaffé, Aniela, 79n

THE COLLECTED WORKS OF
C. G. JUNG

EDITORS: SIR HERBERT READ, MICHAEL FORDHAM, AND GERHARD ADLER; *EXECUTIVE EDITOR*, WILLIAM McGUIRE. *TRANSLATED BY* R.F.C. HULL, EXCEPT WHERE NOTED.

Iɴ ᴛʜᴇ ꜰᴏʟʟᴏᴡɪɴɢ ʟɪsᴛ, dates of original publication are given in parentheses (of original composition, in brackets). Multiple dates indicate revisions.

(*continued*)

The Theory of Psychoanalysis (1913)
General Aspects of Psychoanalysis (1913)
Psychoanalysis and Neurosis (1916)
Some Crucial Points in Psychoanalysis: A Correspondence between Dr. Jung and Dr. Loÿ (1914)
Prefaces to "Collected Papers on Analytical Psychology" (1916, 1917)
The Significance of the Father in the Destiny of the Individual (1909/1949)
Introduction to Kranefeldt's "Secret Ways of the Mind" (1930)
Freud and Jung: Contrasts (1929)

5. SYMBOLS OF TRANSFORMATION ([1911–12/1952] 1956; 2nd edn., 1967)

PART I
Introduction
Two Kinds of Thinking
The Miller Fantasies: Anamnesis
The Hymn of Creation
The Song of the Moth

PART II
Introduction
The Concept of Libido
The Transformation of Libido
The Origin of the Hero
Symbols of the Mother and of Rebirth
The Battle for Deliverance from the Mother
The Dual Mother
The Sacrifice
Epilogue
Appendix: The Miller Fantasies

6. PSYCHOLOGICAL TYPES ([1921] 1971)

A revision by R.F.C. Hull of the translation by H. G. Baynes

Introduction
The Problem of Types in the History of Classical and Medieval Thought
Schiller's Ideas on the Type Problem
The Apollinian and the Dionysian
The Type Problem in Human Character
The Type Problem in Poetry
The Type Problem in Psychopathology

(continued)

(continued)

(*continued*)

16. (*continued*)

The Psychology of the Transference (1946)
Appendix: The Realities of Practical Psychotherapy ([1937] added 1966)

17. THE DEVELOPMENT OF PERSONALITY (1954)
Psychic Conflicts in a Child (1910/1946)
Introduction to Wickes's "Analyses der Kinderseele" (1927/1931)
Child Development and Education (1928)
Analytical Psychology and Education: Three Lectures (1926/1946)
The Gifted Child (1943)
The Significance of the Unconscious in Individual Education (1928)
The Development of Personality (1934)
Marriage as a Psychological Relationship (1925)

18. THE SYMBOLIC LIFE (1954)
Translated by R.F.C. Hull and others

Miscellaneous writings

19. COMPLETE BIBLIOGRAPHY OF C. G. JUNG'S WRITINGS (1976; 2nd edn., 1992)

20. GENERAL INDEX TO THE COLLECTED WORKS (1979)

THE ZOFINGIA LECTURES (1983)
Supplementary Volume A to The Collected Works. Edited by William McGuire, translated by Jan van Heurck, introduction by Marie-Louise von Franz

PSYCHOLOGY OF THE UNCONSCIOUS ([1912] 1992)

A STUDY OF THE TRANSFORMATIONS AND SYMBOLISMS OF THE LIBIDO.
A CONTRIBUTION TO THE HISTORY OF THE EVOLUTION OF THOUGHT

Supplementary Volume B to the Collected Works. Translated by Beatrice M. Hinkle, introduction by William McGuire

Related publications:

THE BASIC WRITINGS OF C. G. JUNG
Selected and introduced by Violet S. de Laszlo

C. G. JUNG: LETTERS
Selected and edited by Gerhard Adler, in collaboration with Aniela Jaffé. Translations from the German by R.F.C. Hull.
VOL. 1: 1906–1950
VOL. 2: 1951–1961

C. G. JUNG SPEAKING: Interviews and Encounters
Edited by William McGuire and R.F.C. Hull

C. G. JUNG: Word and Image
Edited by Aniela Jaffé

THE ESSENTIAL JUNG
Selected and introduced by Anthony Storr

THE GNOSTIC JUNG
Selected and introduced by Robert A. Segal

PSYCHE AND SYMBOL
Selected and introduced by Violet S. de Laszlo

Notes of C. G. Jung's Seminars:

DREAM ANALYSIS ([1928–30] 1984)
Edited by William McGuire

NIETZSCHE'S *ZARATHUSTRA* ([1934–39] 1988)
Edited by James L. Jarrett (2 vols.)

ANALYTICAL PSYCHOLOGY ([1925] 1989)
Edited by William McGuire

THE PSYCHOLOGY OF KUNDALINI YOGA ([1932] 1996)
Edited by Sonu Shamdasani

INTERPRETATION OF VISIONS ([1930-34] 1996)
Edited by Claire Douglas